The Wholehearted Child

PRAISE FOR *THE WHOLEHEARTED CHILD*

"Susan Parker Jones has written a very reasoned, empathic, practical book about children and parenting. She knows the Enneagram well and it clearly informs her therapy practice. Susan has a light-hearted, sensitive touch to her writing. No shaming; just explaining. For parents who want to understand the Enneagram and their children, *The Wholehearted Child* is well worth a read."

-**Jerome Wagner**, Ph.D., Honorary International Enneagram Association Founder

"Susan Parker Jones invites us to experience the wisdom of the Enneagram through the eyes of a primary caregiver or therapist entrusted with a child's wholeness and flourishing. Through children's stories and trauma-informed practices unique to each Enneagram space, she invites us to curiosity, compassion, and action to empower children to become themselves, made in God's image. Susan's heart and skill offer a way to see healthy attachment through harmonious mind, heart, and body wellness. I am thrilled to endorse *The Wholehearted Child* as a unique contribution to the growing body of knowledge called the Enneagram."

-**Rev. Clare Loughrige**, Author ©*iEnneagram, Motions of the Soul,* Coauthor *Spiritual Rhythms for the Enneagram*

"Susan Parker Jones is a true gift to those who know and work closely with her. She can connect with any individual, but especially those who "come from the hard places". Her gentle, calm, and intuitive ability to communicate and navigate emotion from difficult experiences is extraordinary. Her work with the Enneagram and young children is a unique approach and provides parents/caregivers a much deeper perspective, dispelling the myth, "I have tried everything…..nothing works with this child!". *The Wholehearted Child* provides the ability to understand our own childhood, the impact those interactions have on parenting/caregiving, and the ability to develop positive connections with children whose biological nature and/or environmental experience is different than our own. *The Wholehearted Child* and Susan's philosophy of compassionate understanding creates a pathway to supporting and equipping our children for their future."

-**Tammie Benton**, Head Start
State Association Board President

"*The Wholehearted Child* is a perfect book for parents interested in helping their children become their best. Susan Parker Jones provides compassionate advice on how to guide, motivate and discipline children through the most basic and challenging circumstances. Truly a great resource for all parents."

-**Charly George**, Parent

"*The Wholehearted Child* is a groundbreaking resource for parents, educators, and mental health professionals alike. With genuine insight and practical advice, Susan Parker Jones illuminates pathways to nurturing children's emotional resilience and self-awareness through the enneagram. Susan's book is highly impactful and a must-read for anyone seeking to empower children."

-**MacKenzie Davis**, Mental Health Therapist

"If you are looking for a fresh perspective on how to communicate and engage with the next generation, *The Wholehearted Child* is a must-read. As a parent, I know that Susan offers practical strategies to encourage children, validate their feelings, and celebrate their individuality. I know this to be true because these methods are at work in my own home."

-**Andrew Potter**, Parent

"*The Wholehearted Child* is a brilliant resource for anyone looking for an attachment-based, trauma-informed guide to parenting their child well. Susan Parker Jones gives unique insight into child development, and offers specific parenting techniques that cultivate a lasting connection between parent and child. *The Wholehearted Child* is a must-read for every parent!"

-**Kelly Hamilton**, Trauma-Informed Parenting Coach

"*The Wholehearted Child* offers a unique blend of wisdom and modern strategies to help parents raise self-aware, resilient, and compassionate children. Susan Parker Jones provides practical insights and heartfelt guidance, making Susan's book a must-read for any parent looking to foster deep connections and emotional well-being in their children. A truly powerful read!"

-Alexis Schofield, Mental Health Therapist

"More than a parenting manual, *The Wholehearted Child* is a call to embrace the messiness of parenthood with courage and self-compassion. Susan's writing invites us to see parenting as a journey of growth for both ourselves and our children. It's filled with real-life stories and practical strategies that provide renewed hope and clarity for parents."

-Jenny Dedrick - Holistic Coach

"Susan is a treasure to me and my family. Her knowledge and empathy are unmatched. Her words of wisdom have given me comfort and guidance as a mom and I am so grateful she has shared her strategies in *The Wholehearted Child*."

-Jessica Randol, Parent

"Becoming a wholehearted adult begins with a childhood of understanding, nurturing, and empathy. In today's hyper-connected world, it is easy to be disconnected from what is most important, especially during these formative years. Left to chance, without these resources, patterns learned in childhood can follow us decades later, derailing potential and causing unnecessary suffering. In *The*

Wholehearted Child. Susan Parker Jones provides practical wisdom and clear frameworks that will help you know the unique characteristics and challenges for each of your children. An inspiring roadmap to helping you bring out the highest potential in your children and in your relationships with them."

-**Winston Faircloth**, Founder, CEO,
For the Love of Team

"Too many times, we are bombarded with information on how to parent "the right way", that as we try to implement the "right" parenting strategies, we often fail to see our own children as individuals and that there is no one way for all children. *The Wholehearted Child* doesn't focus on how to parent the "right way", but rather providing parents a roadmap to our own self-awareness, providing insights on how our own strengths, challenges, motivations, and fears can influence how we interact with our children and approach parenting. Even better, it helps us develop the skills to support our kids in their own unique journey as we prepare them for their future."

-**Kelly Maurath**, Head Start
Associate Director of Program Services

"Susan Parker Jones has taken her love of children, that she has practiced professionally and personally, and created a manual for healthy parenting. Her knowledge of kids, parents and the enneagram all shine through in these pages. This is not a one size fits all approach, but a fit to each special parent and child personality."

-**Jay Close**, Marriage & Family Therapist

THE
WHOLEHEARTED
CHILD

An Enneagram Informed Guide
to Raising Kind and Confident Kids

Susan Parker Jones

NEW YORK

LONDON • NASHVILLE • MELBOURNE • VANCOUVER

THE WHOLEHEARTED CHILD

An Enneagram Informed Guide to Raising Kind and Confident Kids

For more information and to order additional copies of this title, email info@susanparkerjones.com

For permissions, to order more copies, or to find out about other programs, visit www.susanparkerjones.com

Published in New York, New York, by Morgan James Publishing. Morgan James is a trademark of Morgan James, LLC. www.MorganJamesPublishing.com

Proudly distributed by Publishers Group West®

Morgan James BOGO™

A **FREE** ebook edition is available for you or a friend with the purchase of this print book.

CLEARLY SIGN YOUR NAME ABOVE

Instructions to claim your free ebook edition:
1. Visit MorganJamesBOGO.com
2. Sign your name CLEARLY in the space above
3. Complete the form and submit a photo of this entire page
4. You or your friend can download the ebook to your preferred device

ISBN 9781636985305 paperback
ISBN 9781636985312 ebook
Library of Congress Control Number:
2024940796

Cover Art by:
Vanja Blajic "Miss Belle"

Cover Design by:
Rachel Lopez
www.r2cdesign.com

Interior Design by:
Chris Treccani
www.3dogcreative.net

Edited by:
Darlene Turriff and Nicole Washburn

Morgan James is a proud partner of Habitat for Humanity Peninsula and Greater Williamsburg. Partners in building since 2006.

Get involved today! Visit: www.morgan-james-publishing.com/giving-back

In loving memory of my mother,

Judy Lee Pogorelsky

ACKNOWLEDGMENTS

I am deeply grateful to the following individuals and communities whose guidance, support, and inspiration have been instrumental in shaping this book and my writing journey:

Darlene and Nicole: My dedicated writing coaches, your wisdom and encouragement have been a guiding light throughout this creative process. Your insights and unwavering support have been invaluable.

My Teachers and Guides: Karyn Purvis, Clare and Scott Loughrige, Jerome Wagner, Teresa McCloy, Helen Palmer, Suzanne Stabile, Dan Siegel, Brené Brown, Beatrice Chestnut, and Russ Hudson. Your wisdom and guidance have not only enriched my understanding of healing from life's challenges but have also illuminated the path to my passion for Enneagram-informed parenting.

"Spiritual Rhythms for the Enneagram." This publication is the only one of its kind, entirely dedicated to the Enneagram Harmony Triads. It is a testament to the innovative thinking and profound insights of the authors, Adele & Doug Calhoun and Clare & Scott Loughrige. It is a valuable resource for anyone seeking a deeper understanding of this model.

My Clients: To the parents and children who have trusted me with their stories, your courage and vulnerability have enriched the narrative of this book. You inspire me every day.

Laure Redmond: To my personal coach, Laure Redmond, thank you for being my guiding star on the path to self-discovery. Your wisdom and mentorship have taught me the invaluable process of reclaiming myself.

My loving husband: Drew, you have been my steadfast anchor and the driving force behind my pursuit of becoming the best version of myself. Your unwavering support and belief in me have been my greatest source of strength.

To my children: Allison, Ryan, Michael, Kalkidan, and Gracie. You are my most valuable teachers. Your love and resilience have shaped my perspective on life and the world.

To my parents: You have been my "Butterfly Keepers" and I am forever grateful for the journey that was ours.

This book would not have been possible without your collective influence, encouragement, and expertise. Your contributions have enriched my writing and my appreciation for the power of human connection.

Contents

FOREWORD

As a child, music profoundly influenced my life. It was my voice in the world, a means through which I expressed my energy, creativity, and deepest emotions. Through music, I gained confidence and recognition. As a child, I was unaware of how significantly music was shaping me. Writing and playing music allowed me to articulate my heart's deepest longings, which I later learned to share with others through performance. It was in these early years, of showcasing my talents, that I began to feel my worth was tied to my ability to perform and achieve.

This pattern of seeking validation through performance and recognition persisted into much of my adult life. While it sometimes led to success and accomplishment, more often, it brought pain and disappointment. My fear of failure and relentless pursuit of success often came at the expense of my relationships with those I loved.

My perspective began to shift in my early fifties when I discovered the Enneagram. This tool shed light on my life stories and patterns of thinking, feeling, and behaving. It marked the beginning of a journey away from a tumultuous cycle, following a path God laid out for me. Delving deeper into the Enneagram, I gained insights into my true self. For over ten years, I have methodically unpacked the Enneagram, constantly seeking new ways to explore and understand it.

As my own understanding and experience with the Enneagram has grown and through my journey with life story work, I have seen the connection between the stories we form in us in childhood and the thoughts, feelings and actions we have as adults impact every facet of our lives. But what if we could do it differently and begin earlier to change through stories for our children?

The Wholehearted Child offers a profound new understanding of how we can effectively love and support the next generation. Susan's years of experience working with children as a therapist is evident in this book as she dives deep into the heart of the child. Susan not only teaches us how to nurture the children in our lives but also guides us in reconnecting and reclaiming our own inner child. It's a beautiful experience to read and ponder the threads in your own story and then know that your understanding of self can change the life of a child you love. This book invites you on a journey to weave together the threads of our lives and those of our children, enriching our understanding and connection. Enjoy the exploration that Susan presents in this book, as it holds the potential to enlighten both our children's and our own paths.

Teresa McCloy
(Founder and Creator at the REALIFE Process®)

PREFACE

Creating *The Wholehearted Child* has been a passionate endeavor, driven by the desire to introduce the Enneagram Harmony model, a little-explored yet profoundly illuminating framework for comprehending personality and human behavior. Within the following pages, you are invited to embark on a journey, where we unravel the intricate links between parenting, childhood development, and the Enneagram Harmony Triads.

Before we begin, I would like to express my heartfelt gratitude to those who have played a significant role in validating the Enneagram Harmony model and enriching our understanding of the Enneagram. Their expertise and dedication have been invaluable in shaping the content of this book.

First and foremost, I would like to acknowledge the contributions of those that have come before me. Dr. David Daniels' pioneering work in the Enneagram Harmony model, along with the guidance of Clare and Scott Loughrige, has paved my understanding deeper of the

Enneagram's usefulness in enhancing personal growth and relationships.

I would also like to extend my gratitude to the International Enneagram Association (IEA) Founders for their endorsement of the Enneagram Harmony Triads. Their recognition and support have provided a strong foundation for this work.

The training I've received, ©iEnneagram Motions of the Soul, is accredited by the IEA and led by Clare and Scott Loughrige. It deserves special recognition for being the only International Enneagram Training Program that is entirely Enneagram Harmony Model accredited by the IEA. This accreditation speaks volumes about the credibility and reliability of the Enneagram Harmony model and its practical application.

In this book, my goal is not only to provide insight into the Enneagram Harmony model but also to inspire meaningful change in how we care for ourselves and nurture the next generation. By understanding the Enneagram Harmony Triads and their impact on childhood development, I hope to empower individuals and caregivers to create a more supportive, empathetic, and harmonious future for themselves and their children.

INTRODUCTION

I am one of those people who worries. I mean, I worry a lot. I worry about the climate changing and where all the trash is going. I worry about how dogs feel when they are being dropped off at a shelter and, of course, all the what-ifs. What if there's an earthquake? (I live in Kentucky) What if my husband dies first? (I made him promise not to) and the big one, what if my life as a mom has been an epic fail?

I remember being on the playground in first grade and kids telling me that I was getting a worry line between my eyes and that I better stop, or it would be there forever. FIRST grade!! As a kid, I broke out in hives regularly from worry and then worried if I had caused them. My mom would tell me that my hives wouldn't go away unless I stopped worrying, so I worried about worrying. As my Grandma would say, "OY VEY! Enough already!"

I've learned a lot from being a therapist over the past 25 years, and more importantly, I've traveled my own healing journey as a parent. Yet, the spinning wheel in my head continues its circular whirl, asking: "What have

I passed along to my kids? Have I been a good mom? Did I break the generational patterns that needed to be broken? Will they talk about me in therapy?" This book will help you address these questions and provide you with a means to apply ancient knowledge to your modern parenting challenges.

If you're reading this book, chances are you are someone who understands the deep connection and love parents have for their children and their heartfelt desire to "not mess them up" but to raise happy, confident, and capable adults. For some of us with less-than-perfect childhoods, we have an intense drive to "get it right" with our own kids.

As a parent who is watching her youngest leave the nest, I feel compelled to reach my hand back to the younger parents behind me. I wish I had ALL the answers for you. I don't. What I have is a philosophy and approach derived from attachment theory, childhood development, and an ancient tool that provides insight like no other. In all my experiences and training as a psychotherapist specializing in working with families after trauma and loss, nothing has proven more beneficial than the wisdom I've gleaned using the tool of the Enneagram. As an Attachment Therapist, it makes perfect sense when we consider how mindset is formed. As parents and caregivers, incorporating the Enneagram into our understanding of our children can deepen our connection and support their growth. I will show you how it can shape the way we communicate and guide our kids as we respect their unique qualities and needs. It can also reveal what is relevant to them and what might be showing up for us from our own childhood, giving us insight and strategy to be more intentional and composed.

There is no "one perfect way" to parent or lead kids, but the Enneagram personality analysis tool will give us insight into nine different ways that each of us displays strengths and challenges while parenting.

To make the world a better place for our children, we must commit to raising up a generation to recognize their inherent worth and value. We cannot wait for our kids to be grown to do their healing work. Our children are living in a world that requires them to become equipped to manage the pain it causes them. We must find a way to help kids heal the "hard places" in real-time.

I believe we must teach our wisest, oldest lessons to the youngest, most impressionable among us. While current teachers of the Enneagram rarely, if ever, discuss the Enneagram in conjunction with raising children, I know it is not only possible but hugely beneficial to do so.

My approach works by empowering parents and caregivers, those of us working to change the lives of children through teaching, coaching, and counseling kids, with knowledge about how the journey of childhood shapes the lens we use in adulthood. It is trauma-informed and attachment-oriented, assisting you with the foundational truths about how your children learn to see themselves, others, and the world.

The intention of this book is to provide you with a roadmap for raising self-aware, courageous, and compassionate children. This isn't another book focused on the Enneagram itself but rather a book focused on the sacred role of leading children to emerge into adulthood authentically.

I have loved using the Enneagram as a tool with my adult clients but feel compelled to share it as a parenting guide as well. As over half of my clients are kids between the ages of 6-12, I can't help wanting to point out the trends I am witnessing as a kind of secret key that has the potential to unlock so much clarity for parents and caregivers. I want to invite you to consider using this tool to bring your parenting strategies into focus. You don't need to be concerned with "typing your child" and getting it just right. It's the process of attuning to your child, noticing patterns, and adjusting your guidance that matters. It's also about noticing what is coming up for you in the parent-child relationship and the healing work your childhood may be calling you to do.

Specifically, I will help you guide the children in your life to integrate their three centers of intelligence: head (IQ), heart (EQ), and body (GQ) so that they can begin to master strategies that will lead them to experience self-efficacy, courage, and kindness toward themselves and others. But first, I want to help you learn to do this for yourself.

I hope to equip you with knowledge regarding the complexities of childhood development so that you can better understand your story as well as support the challenges your children face with compassionate understanding. In addition, this book will provide you with insight into personal growth and awareness so that you can be the best and truest version of yourself while raising your child to do the same.

Reading this book will not make you a perfect parent or caregiver. You will continue to make mistakes, as we all do. But if you embrace this journey with courage and curiosity, you will get to the end of your child's childhood with a contented heart that you gave your all. You will rest easier knowing they have the tools they need to face the world with competence and compassion. What I want you to take away from this book is that your parents didn't need to be perfect, and neither do you. It's all practice. Every single day, we do our best and try to live out what we are learning. Stay open, my friend. Stay loving. Fall down. Get up and try again.

It is my hope that this book will serve two purposes: to help you discover truths related to your own child-hood journey and to position you to support your child in theirs. I want you to be able to pause and recognize in real time what is happening for you in your interactions with your child so that you can intentionally care for yourself and them well. I want you to have the insight, skills, and tools to connect with yourself and your child in a way that alleviates shame and post-rage hangovers. I want you to know that you matter and that caring for others without caring for yourself is not sustainable. I want you to factor yourself into the equation and receive some of the energy and care you so generously extend to others. Can you imagine interrupting your automatic pilot, course correcting, and pressing forward to support your child in their journey? Can you hope with me that you can transform your life while guiding your child? Can you dream of a future where you can deeply exhale, knowing you've done your best to equip your child to enter adulthood full of courage, compassion, and wisdom?

As you read this book, I invite you to take your time. Begin reading through the lens of your own childhood journey, just visit the main components, and return to view it a second time through the eyes of a parent. Read and reread it. You can't swallow a steak whole. You must chew it slowly so you can digest it, one bite at a time.

CHAPTER 1

Going Forward by
Looking Back

My parents have a circle driveway that always makes me a bit nervous. If I need to leave and the driveway has other cars, the only way out is going in reverse in an uncomfortable fashion. I find myself holding my breath as I try to maneuver the curve, knowing the only way for me to go home is to go backward.

There are times in life when we all need to look back in order to move forward. We don't want to drive for very long with focus on what's behind us, but it is necessary to inform and position us to get where we need to be. This is one of those times.

There's nothing like raising a child that can trigger our own childhood "hard places" and the dark side of our self-talk and core beliefs. Parenting can serve as a type of mirror that takes us deep into our own reflection. We find that there is a delicate balance between looking back and leading our kids forward. This book will try to strike that balance.

Prior to having children, we may have believed that we knew the path we would take, and it would be different than the one we traveled with our parents. We may have even held several expectations about how our children would be deeply connected, loving, smart, and kind. We envisioned raising them well by being consistent in our nurture, guidance and steadfast love and support.

Most of us start out well, and then one day, as if watching from the audience, we hear sounds coming from our mouths that can't possibly be ours. It sounds like our Mother or Father, Teacher or Coach. It sounds loud and scary and not who we want to be at all. It's a sobering moment. So, we double down. Read all the books and take all the classes. You know, the ones that teach us about parenting, discipline, and what our kids need as a son or daughter. Triggers continue, and we have a nagging feeling that we may have "work to do" regarding our own childhood. Most of us decide to push this 'aha' moment aside and work harder to focus on what our kids need from us right now. It's their turn; after all, we are grown-ups, and it's time to "adult."

Life moves quickly, and now we're just trying to keep up. We've stuck our "inner child" in the basement. We can hear her tantrums from time to time, but we mostly choose to ignore her. Every now and then, we pacify her to keep her quiet, but interacting with her is draining, so most of the time, we don't.

We focus instead on living for our children. Yet, we find that this is not who we planned to be, and this is not the relationship we wanted. Sure, we have some great moments and desperately hope they become our children's core memories. As our kids fall asleep, we pray, "Please, God, let them remember the laughter and not the yelling."

Suits of Armor

Dr. Dan Siegel, renowned Child Psychologist and Author, has a simple saying that carries so much truth. He says, "What's sharable is bearable." When I was very young, I was surrounded by people but often felt alone. In my child mind, there was no one who seemed interested in 'sharing' what I was 'bearing.' My parents had their own thing going on, and, like so many kids, I came to my own conclusions.

Most of us "come to our own conclusions" and build our whole personalities around what we conclude. We discover strategies to help us adapt to the players and scripts we are working with, and though they may be different (humor, anger, perfectionism), they get the job done. Somehow, we survive childhood. I think we wear these strategies like suits of armor until they no longer fit us. And like adults squeezing into teenage jeans, we feel restricted and irritable.

It's about this time that many of us have kids of our own. We may have come to the realization that people were made for connection. We long to raise "our people" without suits of armor that will someday become too small, but in order to raise our children well, we will need to be well.

When we grow up feeling disconnected and unsafe to express our feelings, we learn to misplace them somewhere, either deep inside or onto other people, inadvertently leading our children to do the same. We find ourselves frustrated and unable to become the parent our child requires. As the Apostle Paul lamented, we do the things we don't want to do and find ourselves not doing the things we want to do. We long to give our kids the real strategies they need to become the truest version of themselves. To be people who experience the freedom to move in harmony within themselves and within their relationships. They deserve so much more than just "surviving childhood," and so do we!

But how can we do that for them if we don't know the way ourselves? We can't just put them on a shelf while we travel our own healing journey. No, we are going to have to do both: learn the process of healing ourselves while leading our children with all the tools they will need to do the same. We're going to have to fight from the same side to experience true joy and connection in our families. Hopefully, our children will have a small amount of baggage to unpack when they arrive on the doorstep of adulthood.

Hannah's Story

Hannah found me in her search for an "Enneagram Therapist," and I was so excited. Talking with someone who already knew their "Enneagram type" and wanted to "do the work" seemed like what a sports recruiter must feel when stumbling onto an athlete with raw talent and drive. We wanted the same things and were already speaking the same language.

She told me that she had lost herself in caring for her people, her husband and her daughter, and that she was in the process of rediscovering herself and identifying what brings her joy and how she is impacted by stress. Music to my ears. I love working with clients who are ready to get results and who have a vision for what could be better. "I can get you there!" I said, and like an usher with a flashlight leading a latecomer to their seat in the dark, I thought, "Follow me, it's going to be a great show!"

We worked for several weeks unpacking the tools of my signature program, Wholehearted Connections, and applying them to her self-awareness as well as parenting. So many a-ha moments accompanied by bells and whistles, ohs and ahs, until one day I get a call. "Susan," she said, "I did it!"

Hannah went on to explain that in a tense situation involving her daughter's need for independence and her immediate sense of rejection, which normally would have resulted in tears for both of them, she was able to handle things differently. In real-time, she was able to recognize what was happening for her while also seeing the need beneath the behavior of her child. She went on to explain that in the past, she would have felt rejected and angry and most likely would have lost patience with her 4-year-old. But this time, she cheerfully announced that she was able to catch herself, and then guide and care for herself so that she could guide and care for her daughter. "OMG!!!," I thought, "it's working!!!"

My Story

I wish I had this knowledge while raising my own children. As a Clinical Professional Counselor, I am required to continue receiving education every year to maintain my state licensure and national certification. I have studied to help me counsel and train others as I've taught as an Adjunct Professor, Workshop Leader, and Keynote Speaker. I've learned a lot. One thing I know for sure is that theory is much different than application. There is "head knowledge" and "rubber meets the road skill."

I was brought to my knees by the required skill it took to raise two of my children after adopting them at ages 5 and 7 from Ethiopia. One day, I found myself in exhaustion and despair. Weeks of not speaking the same language, collecting poop for parasite screenings, my children's fascination with seeing what would go down the drains, coloring on walls, hoarding of food in windowsills, and constant screaming whenever we drove anywhere because they felt trapped in their seat belts, had taken its toll.

At my wit's end, I reached out to the Center for Child Development at Texas Christian University, now called the Karyn Purvis Child Development Institute, where I received training from Dr. Purvis to provide TBRI or Trust-Based Relational Intervention. "I am overwhelmed and lost!" I cried to the Counselor on the other end of the phone.

She patiently asked me a few questions to assess my knowledge of the situation. I could tell by her tone that she was somewhat taken aback as my responses didn't match my emotional state. She replied, "Wow, you have a good understanding of trauma and attachment. Do you happen to have an Attachment Therapist in your area?"

Silence. Tears.

Me: "I AM the Attachment Therapist in my area."

My "head knowledge" often aligned with my inner critic and beat me up with shame that I wasn't doing this parenting gig quite right. It had been so easy with my older children. I was in over my head, but I didn't need more lessons on attachment theory or how kids respond after trauma. What I needed was a greater understanding of how to manage what was happening in me while I tried to create a safe place for my kids to manage what was happening in them, which was curiosity and excitement mixed with a lot of fear and confusion.

My children had spent years in an orphanage where they were abused and confined. They experienced a car, an airplane, and snow, all for the first time within days of meeting me. They were given beautiful bunk beds, which they quickly abandoned for the floor, and new toys, which they instantly destroyed. They were eating different foods and living with a family that didn't look, talk, or behave like anyone else they had known. I wanted to nurture, protect, and love them, and they looked at me like I was a crazy lady. I felt defeated and alone and deeply triggered that I was doing something wrong that was impacting my whole family.

I have spent the last 15 years learning and experimenting with balancing theory and application. I have been blessed with clients who have been willing to share in my excitement and creative exploration until we landed on something solid for both the children and their caregivers. It is the same work. Parents just need to do it while simultaneously guiding their children. It's tricky, but there is so much ease when you lay down your resistance.

The benefit to you as you apply what I am about to share in this book is clarity. Will all your struggles be removed in some kind of parenting Utopia? Nope. But will you know the dragon you're fighting and how to tame it? Absolutely. When you can recognize the real battle you're facing and have the strategies to do it well, you save so much precious energy. You also gain so much success in the adventure of parenting, which is measured not by winning every argument but by staying connected, grounded, and true to the person you want to be, so your child gets the parent they need.

Your clarity will bring confidence and connection in a way that is invaluable and necessary for the paving of your child's path to preventative mental health and wellness. You have but a few short years to make an impact of a lifetime for your kids and the rest of your life to wonder if you got it right. The question is similar to the one posed by Mary Oliver when she writes, "Tell me, what is it you wish to do with your ONE, wild and precious life?" I would add, "And how will you help your child live theirs?"

CHAPTER 2

The Stories We Tell

When I was in Kindergarten, I became very ill and had to stay in the hospital for several weeks following an emergency surgery. I remember feeling really scared and alone. In those days, parents were only allowed during visiting hours. I recall my father visiting and playing "Ants in the Pants" with me. This game required little conversation as we pressed the backs of play ants, making them fly with the hope that they would land in a pair of plastic pants. I don't recall anyone else visiting me, though most likely they did, and I don't remember anyone taking the time to explain my situation. Instead, I remember the story I told myself, that I was too much to care for and that I was on my own. It was a story that invited fear and unworthiness as unwanted companions well into my adulthood.

For me, this unworthiness gave birth to a general sense of uncertainty. I was rarely able to trust my instincts or inner "knowing", which gave space for my Inner Critic to be steadfast with suggestions of "try harder" or suffer rejection and judgment. Like a father, my insecurity walked me down the aisle to a marriage that I sustained for 23 years through a "think happy thoughts" and "love keeps no record of wrongs" kind of mindset. My "Sun Will Come Out Tomorrow" anthem of denial helped push away pain and heartbreak until my body, which was holding all of it, let the truth out in one magnificent crash.

The "Hard Places" of Childhood

I want to share with you a bit of background to all the things that contribute to a child's development. Not because you need more "theory" but to understand that there are so many factors, we can't always control, that

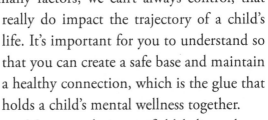

really do impact the trajectory of a child's life. It's important for you to understand so that you can create a safe base and maintain a healthy connection, which is the glue that holds a child's mental wellness together.

Most people in my field believe that a child's "mindset," or template from which they view the world, is formed by the time they hit school age and that the first 5 years are the most important. Even if a child is born to the most idyllic parents, Attachment Theorists have identified several early risk factors that can cast a shadow on a child's path to a healthy and secure attachment, potentially leading to difficulties in navigating stress later. Dr. Karyn Purvis, creator and co-author of *The Connected Child,* coined these risk factors as the "hard places" of childhood. They include the following:

- **Prenatal Stress/Trauma:** When caregivers experience stress or trauma during pregnancy, it can impact the emotional environment even before a child is born. This can lay the groundwork for potential attachment struggles, as a child may enter the world unsettled and anxious.

- **Traumatic or Difficult Birth factor:** This stormy entry into the world can leave kids feeling a bit disoriented and overwhelmed. A traumatic birth experience can set the stage for emotional challenges, making it a bit harder for a child to establish secure connections with their caregivers, causing their "lens" to be skewed.

- **Early Hospitalization:** Separation from caregivers in the case of hospitalization, especially when it involves painful medical procedures or extended stays, can create a sense of detachment and insecurity in a child that can alter their natural developmental trajectory.

- **Neglect or Loss of Caregiver:** When a child doesn't receive the consistent care and attention they need from their primary caregivers, it can leave a lasting impact on their attachment style. Additionally, the loss of a caregiver through divorce, death, or separation can lead to feelings of intense grief, abandonment, and insecurity.

- **Abuse:** Lastly, we must face the reality of abuse, which can leave deep scars on young hearts and minds. Experiencing abuse, whether physical, emotional, or sexual, can severely impact a child's ability to form secure attachments and can lead to disorganized and fearful responses in relationships.

Of course, there can be many "hard places" along the road of childhood, resulting in developmental trauma that kids endure along the journey. I am always so grateful to parents for recognizing the value and benefit of counseling rather than buying into the myths, as so many do that keep their kids locked in pain and false beliefs for years.

Myths Related to Kids

None of us want to see our kids in pain, but too often, we jump to fix it or deny our child's suffering altogether. We say things like, "You're okay," to reassure them and ourselves that this discomfort is temporary. The myth we believe is that somehow, if our child is in pain, we have failed. We don't want our kids to hurt, and we definitely don't want to make things worse as parents. Instead, we wish we had a fast-forward button to propel them, and us, to the other side of pain. We hope that somehow, if we tiptoe around it, it will just all fade away. The true failure is, not that our child has experienced pain, but that we have left them alone to face it.

I often hear parents tell me they don't want to 'rock the boat' and that their child seems fine even in the face of tragic loss or unbearable heartbreak. Kids, especially those who have suffered the "hard places," are good at scanning their environment to adapt to the room. We must not be quick to think that, just because they aren't sharing their pain in an obvious way, means they aren't feeling it.

Some people believe that "time will heal all wounds," and this is simply not true. The impact of loss and trauma doesn't just "go away." Kids don't "grow out of it" or forget the lessons they infer from it. As parents, we need to create a safe place for children to bring it into the light so we can face it together. By doing so, we help kids learn they can reach higher ground and safeguard their 'true' selves in connection to their innate intelligence: head, heart, and body and to those who love them.

We can feel uncomfortable when our children are in distress. All too often, we jump to "fixing" their problems or convincing them that they don't really have one. What if instead we held space with them in a manner that said, "This is hard, but you and I can do hard things together."

Now, at this point, you may be wondering, Do I even know all the things my child may need to heal from? Your mind may be revisiting their storyline and thinking, "Did I miss something?" I can almost feel that "What if" wheel beginning to spin in your head. Take a deep breath. Relax. What I am attempting to do is help you see the small "tells" that something may be off and that your child may be experiencing stress and believing untruths.

Not all healing work happens in the counseling relationship. Counselors don't have a magic wand that heals the hearts of children, though I often wish we did. We can't gain much ground without parental involvement. The real healing happens with you. When you recognize and understand who your child is meant to be in their full, true expression, you will also be able to note when they are presenting their "false" or adaptive self, indicating that they are in stress. This is your invitation to connection and the space where you will do your best coaching as a parent.

Myths Related to Parents and Caregivers

As parents and caregivers, we also must recognize the myths that restrain our own healing and growth. Too often, we mistake "happy" for "whole" and "self-care" with "self-indulgence." While Netflix and a glass of wine may feel like "self-care," it may only serve as a numbing out instead of an honest process of recognizing and attending to our pain.

Depending on our personality type, we can get caught up in our own thinking loops, anger outbursts, or depressive withdrawals. Without intentional awareness, our patterns of thinking, feeling, and behaving can dictate how we navigate life as half asleep and numbed or amped up and stressed out. Waking up and staying present for ourselves and our kids is the first step in living and leading them well.

As parents and caregivers, we have the arduous task of navigating our own "hard places" while leading children to do the same. Though we may have endured shared heartbreak, such as divorce or loss, a child's story and perspective are different from ours. We must find a way to relay the message that we are with them in the painful battle for their peace and identity. No matter when we enter their story, they need to know the fight is not theirs to do alone, and we are on their side. In the coming chapters, you will learn about personality types and how to navigate what it means to get to the place Hanna did with your very own "aha" moment.

As you lead the children in your life, consider helping them be **TRUE** to themselves as they **T**rust their centers of intelligence, build strategies for **R**esilience while honoring their **U**nique needs, and hold **E**mpathy for themselves and others. This strategy will move your child along in having a wholehearted mindset and pave a path for preventative mental wellness.

Stages and Changes

Experienced parents can tell you that just when you think you have it down, your children's needs change. You finally feel competent and hit your stride, and suddenly, your child's journey presents new challenges, and your parenting job description gets rewritten. Each of us went through stages and changes as kids, and our parents may or may not have navigated them well. To help us understand the challenge, let's look at another theory.

Around the same time Attachment Theory was being formed by John Bowlby, another hypothesis on human development was being proposed by Erik Erikson.

Erikson proposed that all of us go through stages of psychosocial development, each characterized by a unique conflict or challenge that must be successfully resolved for healthy development to occur. For our purposes, we are going to look at stages related to infancy through adolescence. I believe this insight will provide you with greater understanding and compassion for the challenges facing your child that may give rise to "stinky behaviors" and damaging beliefs. When you know the "task at hand" it may provide you with a kind of target to aim for, allowing you to be more intentional and less reactive in your approach.

- **Trust vs. Mistrust (Infancy, 0-1 year):** During the first year of life, infants develop a sense of trust in their caregivers and the world around them, as noted in Attachment Theory. A responsive and nurturing caregiver fosters a foundation of trust, while neglect or inconsistency may lead to feelings of mistrust and insecurity. This stage is foundational to all other emotional and relational growth and development.

- **Autonomy vs. Shame and Doubt (Toddlerhood, 1–3 years):** As toddlers explore their independence, they face the challenge of asserting their autonomy. Encouraging a safe environment for exploration allows children to develop a sense of self-control and confidence. Overly strict or critical parenting can lead to a child's shame and doubt in their abilities. In this stage, parents and kids benefit from "shared control," allowing kids to choose when feasible and teaching them to find their voice within boundaries.

- **Initiative vs. Guilt (Preschool, 3–6 years):** Preschoolers become more curious and eager to take on new challenges. Supporting their initiative and creativity fosters a sense of purpose and initiative. However, overly controlling or discouraging behavior can lead to feelings of guilt and insecurity. In this stage, caregivers help children learn to express themselves, providing them with encouragement to try new things and get comfortable making mistakes as part of the learning process.

- **Industry vs. Inferiority (School Age, 6–11 years):** During middle childhood, children develop a sense of competence and accomplishment through mastering new skills. Encouragement and positive feedback from parents and teachers foster feelings of industry and confidence. Conversely, a lack of support can result in a sense of inferiority and insecurity. In this case, children may struggle with self-esteem, which can impact their mental health, social relationships, and school performance.

- **Identity vs. Role Confusion (Adolescence, 12–18 years):** In this stage, Adolescents grapple with questions of identity and self-discovery.

This time is all about figuring out who they are independently from their parents and family. Successfully navigating this stage involves forming a clear and coherent sense of self and future aspirations. Failure to do so may result in feeling lost and confused about themselves and their place in the world.

You don't need to be a Psychotherapist to be a great parent, but understanding Erikson's theories is crucial because it provides us with valuable insights into our needs and those of our children at different stages of life. With this knowledge, we may be more equipped to apprehend our stories and our reactions to them. We can hold greater compassion and understanding for the self-talk and responses that are authored by our 'inner child,' hopefully with the insight to re-parent this part of us well.

Healthy parenting is focused on "front-loading" your relationship with your child with permission, language, signals, and invitations to connect. Knowing what all kids have in common regarding their development helps you better understand the milestones they are working toward. Thankfully, we are only working with one stage at a time, and even when we have multiple children, a few tools can go a long way. Let's get started.

CHAPTER 3

The Wholehearted

I've always loved the word "Wholehearted" as I serve the "Brokenhearted." After discovering the work of Brené Brown, the word inspired me even further. As a researcher, Dr. Brown discovered that people who had qualities that supported authentic living had a foundational core belief that they were "brave and worthy of love and belonging." She gave them the label of "wholehearted."

I am sharing with you my approach that is founded on the belief that recovering from the "hard places" requires intentional care to protect and nurture a child's strengths as they grow true to their wholehearted design and calling. I call these parents and caregivers the "Butterfly Keepers" because their work is to ensure the emergence of the innate brilliance and beautiful giftings of those in their care.

Dr. Brown's book, The Gifts of Imperfection, inspired me so much that I lean on her guideposts heavily as both a clinician and, more importantly, as a "Butterfly Keeper." I have adapted them as a kind of target to aim for, though as a mom, I often miss the mark. When I do, these statements or promises help bring me home to myself. You may find them helpful, too! They are the following:

- **Be True to Myself:** It's about embracing who I really am and ditching the need to be perfect or please everyone. I've learned that authenticity means being genuine and honest about who I am.

- **Show Self-love and Compassion:** Treating myself with kindness and understanding, like I would with a dear friend. I remind myself that I am absolutely worthy of love and belonging at all times.

- **Bounce Back Stronger:** Resilience is key. Life's full of challenges and disappointments, but I've learned to bounce back from setbacks and failures, understanding they're opportunities for growth and meaningful lessons.

- **Embrace Gratitude and Joy:** I try to make it a routine to focus on things to be grateful for and mindfully enjoy the moments that bring me joy. It's all about finding beauty in everyday life and being thankful for it.

- **Trust My Gut:** I trust my intuition and have faith in myself and God, even when things seem out of control. It's all about trusting my inner wisdom and instincts.

- **Nurture Creativity:** Creativity is a big part of my life. I make time for creative expression because it's a wonderful way to feed my soul and find my joy.
- **Play and Rest:** I've learned to prioritize play and rest. They're essential for my well-being, and I make sure to indulge in activities that bring me back to me.
- **Create Moments of Calm:** In the busyness of life, I create moments of calm and stillness. These times of reflection and mindfulness help me find peace and clarity.
- **Meaningful Work:** Meaningful work is essential. I seek opportunities that align with my values and give me a sense of purpose. It's how I find fulfillment and connection.
- **Laughter, Song, and Dance:** Joy and fun are non-negotiable. I carve out time to dance every single week because it brings me back to myself.
- These promises help us to remember we are human, just like our kids. We all do better when we slow down and live with intention. They help us practice living "on purpose" with self-compassion and deeper connections with ourselves and others. These are the truths that we must share with our children.

Ennea What?

So, what exactly is the Enneagram anyway and what does it have to do with being wholehearted? This tool is a powerful personality system that has gained popularity in recent years for its ability to provide deep insights into human behavior, motivations, and growth. With roots dating back centuries, the Enneagram has evolved into a comprehensive framework for understanding personality 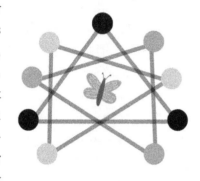 dynamics and promoting personal development.

The history of the Enneagram can be traced to ancient spiritual traditions, including Christianity and various mystical teachings. However, it was modern psychologists and teachers who brought the Enneagram into mainstream consciousness during the 20th century and a new generation that exploded the Enneagram on social media in recent years.

If you're not familiar, let me share a brief explanation. The Enneagram comes from the Greek word, "ennea" meaning nine and "gram" meaning drawing and you will often see it depicted as nine points around a circle. These nine points represent nine distinct personality types, each representing different patterns of thinking, feeling, and behaving. These types are interconnected by a complex web of relationships, highlighting both the strengths and challenges of each type.

The Enneagram goes beyond simply categorizing people into personality types; it offers a deep understanding of the underlying motivations, fears, and needs that drive our actions. It is a teacher of personal growth and transformation, helping its students to recognize and break free from self-limiting patterns and develop healthier ways of living. So, what does this have to do with parenting a wholehearted child, you ask? The answer is EVERYTHING.

The Three Informants

As we travel the path toward raising healthy kids, we can remember that we were created for the journey. The best way I describe it when I work with children is that we have "three informants" that let us know how we are doing and help us navigate the hard places of life. They are our thinking head, feeling heart, and sensing body. Children learn that each "Informant" provides valuable information about their experiences and can guide them back to being their best selves.

With this newfound awareness, we can guide children to express their thoughts, emotions, and bodily sensations with descriptive language. Through creative exercises, they can learn to articulate their needs, allowing them to voice their questions and choices assertively and respectfully. We can empower them to communicate their emotional states, facilitating deeper connections with caregivers and peers and fostering a sense of emotional safety.

By helping children recognize and honor the wisdom of their thoughts, emotions, and physical sensations, we empower them to develop and become the best versions of themselves. While this may appear too lofty for children to grasp, I can share that from experience; even preschoolers can get on board when we are creative in our approach.

As we will explore, the Enneagram is centered around nine personality types, but we are NOT aiming to type our children or put them in a so-called "box." Rather, we are looking for ways to respond to our children's behavior with compassion and a greater curiosity of what may be driving it. The tool of the Enneagram can inform us how to discern the emerging traits our children may be displaying so we can help them grow true to their strengths and innate gifts, as well as help them grow in self-awareness as they learn to trust themselves, build resilience, appreciate their uniqueness and hold empathy for themselves and others.

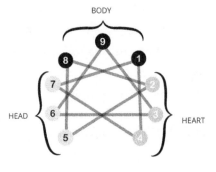

The Enneagram incorporates the concept of our informants as our three centers of intelligence, suggesting different ways that people perceive themselves and process information. I will explain the "types" soon, but for now, take note of the following:

- The Head Center: This center is associated with thinking and processing information intellectually. Types 5, 6, and 7 are part of the Head Center.
- The Heart Center: This center is linked to emotional processing and interpersonal relationships. Types 2, 3, and 4 are part of the Heart Center.
- The Body Center: This center is associated with physical sensations and instincts. Types 8, 9, and 1 are part of the Body Center.

Through practices such as mindfulness, reflection, and cultivating playful awareness, we can guide our children in developing a deep connection with these three centers, enabling them to navigate the world with greater self-understanding, empathy, and confidence.

Little I, Big Difference

After years of study, I've learned that the Enneagram is not a simple tool like a hammer. Rather, it's a multifaceted tool, like a Swiss Army Knife, offering surprise after surprise with so many ways to apply its usefulness.

I was first introduced to the Enneagram as a young therapist 25 years ago. At that time, I struggled to understand its relevance as my work was focused on children. Many years later, I was reintroduced to it through the work of Jerome Wagner and Clare and Scott Loughrige. In their *Motions of the Soul Practitioner* training, Clare and Scott presented the iEnneagram, and finally, things began to click for me.

The little "i" in iEnneagram stands for Ignatius, as in Saint Ignatius of Loyola, who was the founder of the Jesuit Order. St. Ignatius is not directly associated with the development of the Enneagram theory but did contribute significantly to the field of spiritual development and self-awareness through his work on the Spiritual Exercises. His teachings emphasize self-examination, discernment, and deep reflection on one's motivations and desires. His integration of spiritual and psychological insights offers a more holistic approach to personal development and a deeper connection to one's authentic self and spiritual journey. Sounds a bit heavy for a parenting book? Keep reading, friend.

The Harmony Triads

As we dive a little deeper into St. Ignatius' Harmony Triad Model, we find that he highlights the interplay between the three centers of intelligence: the head, the heart, and the body. St. Ignatius argued 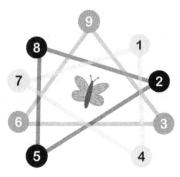 that we were each created in the image of a triune God and, therefore, should consider ourselves as triune beings. Though most learn about the Enneagram with recognition of one type as primary, under this theory, we have two other types that can inform us as we embrace harmony-based living. The Harmony Triads are as follows:

- Triad 1-4-7 (Body 1, Heart 4, Head 7)
- Triad 2-5-8 (Heart 2, Head 5, Body 8)
- Triad 3-6-9 (Heart 3, Head 6, Body 9)

As a therapist, with a passion for serving kids, I am confident that this theory fits with the fluidity of child development. Also, the hope of integrating one's Head, Heart, and Body Intelligence is a goal of healers and child-care workers across many disciplines. The fact that schools provide free lunch programs to their students indicates that even school district leaders know nourishing a child's physical body results in greater emotional well-being and intellectual success.

Why it Matters

We can all benefit from acknowledging that the interplay between our three centers of intelligence exists and integrating these centers will help us pave a path of preventative wellness in ourselves and our kids.

By understanding and harmonizing the Head, Heart, and Body centers, we gain a more holistic perspective on our thoughts, emotions, and actions. This integration allows us to approach challenges with greater clarity, empathy, and effectiveness. We become better equipped to manage stress, make thoughtful decisions, and cultivate deeper connections with others.

Meet Addie

Addie was adopted as a toddler after being removed from her parents after severe neglect. She was referred to me for help with her tremendous need to be in control of everything, especially her food intake, from a position of insecurity. After much work, I was relieved to hear her report back to me that a slumber party had gone well for her. She explained that upon seeing food and experiencing the panicked impulse to gorge, she calmed her body by breathing and, with a hand on her chest, spoke to her feeling heart, reminding it that she was safe, and gently confronted her thinking brain to help it remember there is plenty to go around. She was so proud of herself and beamed with confidence that she had remembered our practice and put it to use when it counted.

For our children, this integration fosters emotional intelligence, resilience, and self-awareness from a young age, providing them with invaluable tools to navigate life's heartbreaks and challenges. As parents, we can support our children in exploring and balancing these centers, encouraging them to develop a well-rounded and compassionate approach to themselves and the world around them. Ultimately, the integration of the three centers of intelligence empowers both us and our kids to emerge as our best "butterfly" selves with our strengths and gifts intact.

CHAPTER 4

Free to Be You and Me

I'm 8 years old and lying on a soft oriental rug singing along to "Free to Be You and Me," playing on a little blue record player that resembles a suitcase. My blonde hair hangs from two ponytails and pools on the floor against the deep reds and golds of the carpet. I'm at my friend Marion's house, and we have been given dominion of this space for the night. With its oak paneled walls and access to the kitchen, it is perfect for two third graders who want to sing and "nosh" the night away from what feels like miles from other family members.

For those of you who didn't grow up in the 70s, let me explain. "Free to Be... You and Me" is an iconic children's album released in 1972. It was created by Marlo Thomas from *That Girl* and her friends, including well-known artists such as Alan Alda, Mel Brooks, and Diana Ross. The album featured a collection of songs, poems, and stories that promoted messages of gender equality, self-expression, and acceptance. As children listening, we were encouraged to embrace our uniqueness, to dream big, and to be kind. Some of my favorite songs were "William has a Doll" and "It's All Right to Cry," and I loved giggling with Marion as we listened to a conversation between two babies on gender roles.

I purchased the album years later for my own children and continue to hold onto the dream that someday we will live in a land where "you and me are free to be you and me." What I know now is that it will take some inner work to get ourselves there and a lot of intentionality to bring our children along.

Mixed Messages

From an early age, many of us received mixed messages. We were told we are "free to be" and told to conform. Whether said directly or not, many of us heard, "You're not good enough." "Don't question authority." and "You are too talkative, too emotional, too assertive, and too silly."

Rather than living from a "Free to be Me" Self, we have been forced to live from a "Conform to Survive Self." In my profession, we call these our "Authentic" and "Adaptive" selves or "True" and "False" selves. Whatever you call them, the Conformer/Adaptor/False self, they are just terms to describe our Ego at work. It adapts to our childhood "hard places" and becomes like a suit of armor that both protects and restricts us as we grow into adulthood. It will take a lot of courage to remove it, stripping down in courage and vulnerability, to be free to be you and me. It's not for everyone. It's scary. It takes strength and a willingness to hope for something more. You can do it, Friend, and I promise you will experience so much more freedom on the other side!

The goal of our "inner work" is not to destroy our "Adaptive" qualities but rather to transform them as we employ curiosity and self-compassion, knowing that these qualities have served a purpose in our lives. We want to notice, without judgment, when we find ourselves grappling with emotions such as fear, shame, and anger, as they typically inspire us to do our best adaptive tap dance to avoid the hook of rejection and pain.

As parents, we want to train our children to be in tune with themselves as well. We want to teach them early to be aware of who they are when they are feeling free to be themselves and who they become when they don't. Of course, we want to raise our children to have manners and self-control- this isn't free-for-all parenting or an excerpt from *The Lord of the Flies*. The goal is to help them know and protect the brilliance they were innately born within a world that would quickly compel them to dim their light.

This work helps each of us recognize and honor our "true" authentic self, avoiding a lifetime of compensating patterns and false beliefs. It's about knowing where we each go in times of stress, revealing the lies we believe, and the hope that pushes us along to live intentionally as our authentic, best self. Our shared goal is to gather our children and raise the next generation with tools for self-awareness, courage and the gift of knowing they are worthy of love and belonging. It's going to require patience, intentionality, and our own self-awareness. The best tool we have to assist us is the Enneagram.

The Nine Types

There is so much more to the Enneagram: wings, stances, instinctual subtypes, to name a few. If your interest is sparked, there is more for you to look forward to learning. For now, let's stay on course. To get started, let's look at a brief description of each of the nine types. These are generalities, and there is so much more to show you. Stay with me; we'll get a closer view later.

I want to share a brief overview of each type, and as most Enneagram teachers do, I'm going to use numerals and start at the top of the graph with the "body-centered types."

- **Type 8–The Challenger:** Individuals that type as 8 are motivated by their need for control and protection. They fear being controlled or harmed, so they assert themselves and take charge of situations to avoid vulnerability. They are known for being strong-willed and protective of their loved ones.

- **Type 9–The Peacemaker:** Those who type as a 9 are generally motivated by their desire for inner and outer peace. They fear conflict and disconnection, so they often avoid confrontation and seek harmony. They are known for providing a sense of calm and are accommodating to maintain a sense of peace in their relationships.

- **Type 1–The Improver:** People with traits of type 1 are motivated by their desire to be good, right, and moral. They have a strong internal critic and seek perfection in themselves and others. They believe that by following the rules and doing things "the right way," they can create a more orderly and just world.

- **Type 2–The Helper:** Individuals with Type 2 qualities are motivated by their need to be needed and loved. They derive their self-worth from helping and caring for others. They fear being unimportant or unloved, so they go out of their way to be generous and supportive.

- **Type 3–The Achiever:** People who type as a 3 are typically motivated by their desire for success and recognition. They fear being worthless or unimportant, so they strive to excel in their pursuits and gain admiration from others. They are known for being ambitious and driven to achieve their goals.

- **Type 4–The Individualist:** Generally, Type 4 individuals are motivated by their search for identity and significance. They fear being ordinary or insignificant, so they cultivate their unique self-expression and emotions. They are in touch with their feelings and often experience a range of emotions deeply.

- **Type 5–The Investigator:** People with Type 5 traits are motivated by their need for knowledge and understanding. They fear being overwhelmed or seen as incapable, so they often withdraw into their mind to conserve energy and protect themselves from the demands of the world.

- **Type 6–The Loyalist:** Those who type as a 6 are motivated by their need for security and guidance, and because of this, they seek certainty and reassurance from authority figures and groups. They are vigilant and can be anxious about potential risks. They also have a "counter type" that pushes through their anxiety to do the thing they fear.

- **Type 7–The Enthusiast:** Generally, Type 7 individuals are motivated by their desire for new experiences and freedom. They fear being deprived or trapped, so they avoid pain and negative emotions by seeking pleasure and novelty. They are known for being spontaneous and optimistic.

So, you are probably wondering, "How will I know?" Cue Whitney. My guess is that your focus has gone to your kids and your parenting. Let's bring it back to you for a minute. Not you, the parent. Just you, the person. Stay curious and stay open.

There are several ways to discern your Enneagram type and many more lessons to glean from other sources. As adults, we can take a variety of quizzes or assessments to suggest our type. Perhaps you already have your type in mind as you hold this book. If you do, I invite you to adopt a "learner's mind" and stay open. If not, please follow along and trust the journey. Like a photographer adjusting their lens, you will find your Enneagram landscape sharpened into breathtaking clarity.

CHAPTER 5
Ego Dragons

What You Need to Know

If we continue our quest to understand the influence of our care as parents and caregivers, as well as childhood "hard places" in the shaping of who we become, we would be wise to consider the creation of the ego, also known as our sense of self, which is intricately connected to navigating stages of development and our attachment experiences.

A secure attachment fosters positive ego development, where a child feels valued, loved, and worthy of care. This healthy ego serves as a foundation for self-esteem, confidence, and emotional regulation throughout life. Kids who experience this positive ego development typically stay on a steady course to their authentic or "real" selves.

On the other hand, insecure attachment experiences, such as neglect, abuse, or inconsistent caregiving, may develop defense mechanisms or coping strategies that impact their self-image and self-worth. This leads to the formation of a fragile or maladaptive ego, or as I call it, their "dragon."

These early attachment experiences significantly shape the ego and lay the groundwork for how children view themselves and connect to others. Kids who experience injuries to their attachment formation learn how to alter themselves and adapt to their environments. It is as if they were assigned a well-meaning but domineering dragon who continually disrupts their divine trajectory. Misguided and confused, their dragon attempts to protect the child but instead tears their wings and hinders them from taking flight.

It's Simply Complicated

Now, life is more complicated than "all or nothing" or being fully authentic or altogether adaptive. We are complex beings. Few, if any, of us have had perfect childhoods, and most, if not all of us, live from a combination of our authentic and adaptive traits. All of us have maladaptive "ego dragons" to contend with.

Though we may want to follow a path to wholehearted living, it is seldom easy to stay on course. We each have a dragon, though some are fiercer than others. Our way of living in the world is so deeply ingrained in our experiences of it that we rarely notice what parts are real and what parts are false. We internalize our dragon and believe it to be a truth teller when in fact, it is not. We sabotage ourselves with doubt; we overeat, withdraw from support, or we yell at those we love-all things to signal that the dragon is at the helm, and we are adrift. We're simply misguided people doing the best we can to make sense of the world around us.

As a counselor and someone who has been through her own heartbreak, I can tell you that it typically takes a kind of "dark night of the soul" to cause the scales to drop from our eyes. We just don't see how far we've drifted into the shadows with our dragons until the cave begins to crumble, and the light reveals the truth.

Achieving the ability to grow true to ourselves is not about seeking perfection but about embracing our beautifully imperfect selves with love and acceptance. Our dragon cannot be slain. We must learn to tame it while honoring all aspects of our being, acknowledging the vulnerability as a sign of strength, and realizing that growth is an ever-unfolding process. Our dragon roars, and instead of reacting, we learn to respond bravely with love, gentleness, and courage. We take our dragon for a walk. We calm them and thank them for trying to protect us with firm reassurance that our wiser self has it from here.

Our Words

Too often, parents come to my waiting room with a mile-long list of what their children are doing wrong. "He's rude." "She's dramatic." "He is disrespectful and controlling." "She lies and hoards food." The list of complaints goes on and on. As a parent, I understand the desperation to vent and be understood. The need to have someone else say, "You're not crazy," is fierce. We know our words are powerful and can be used to build up or tear down, but the struggle is real. So, where can we begin?

Kids are smart, but we're not going to be able to have conversations with them about how they're showing up as their "Adaptive Self" versus their "Authentic Self." They will most likely look at us like we have two heads if we do.

We want to be mindful that we are speaking to them in a way that helps them move the needle in the right direction. As parents and caregivers, we want their chrysalis development to go well. We will get more of what we pay attention to, and we want to "get more" of the good stuff.

We need to teach them to know when their dragon is present and to move with courage in another direction. It will be our sacred role as "Butterfly Keepers" to help them emerge from the cave and spread their wings.

Felt Safety

To help kids develop into the best version of themselves, we must first create a sense of "felt safety." We can know that a child is safe in our care, but unless we create an environment that allows them to feel safe, a child will be in full defense mode, and their dragon will be in charge. This means that we are mindful of our voice, its cadence, tone, and volume. It means that we are gentle and kind and approach our children with curiosity and compassion.

When they do something wrong, we meet them mindfully saying, "I wonder…" or "Can you help me understand…?" and not "What's wrong with you?!" It means that we check in with ourselves and respect our own tendencies when reacting to chaos and stress. Creating "felt safety" for kids means that we create a safe environment for each of us to recognize and meet our needs when experiencing anger, fear, or shame in any form. It also means that we remain hopeful, pointing them and ourselves to what's possible.

As we nurture their chrysalis, we want to help our kids get a vision for their potential. We do this by noticing and reflecting on their emerging brilliance and authentic expression of strength, love, and wisdom. We point them to other "butterflies" in the world, their role models in teachers, leaders, and family members, that reflect who they might become in all their future colorful displays. Creating "felt safety" means that we use our words to speak life over our kids, reminding them of all that's already there.

They need to know that we are not on opposing sides. The fight is not against them or their snarky behavior; it is against the dragons who want to shatter and mold them in a way that damages their wings and destroys their brilliant colors. We must teach them to recognize these beasts as Fear, Shame, and Anger and give them strategies to meet them with curiosity, courage and self-compassion.

Emerging Enneagram Types in Kids

I use the term "emerging" when studying the Enneagram in children because it acknowledges that their personality or Enneagram type is still developing and evolving. Children are in a continuous process of self-discovery and growth, and their Enneagram type may not be fully formed or apparent at a young age. By using the term "emerging," we recognize that children's personalities are dynamic and subject to change as they navigate various life experiences and develop their own unique perspectives. It allows us to approach the study of Enneagram types in children with a sense of openness, curiosity, and amenability. This term reminds us to be mindful of the fluidity and potential for growth within each child, honoring their individual journeys and supporting their development with understanding and compassion.

Recognizing the dominant emerging Enneagram types in children can provide valuable insights into their unique personalities and needs. While children's Enneagram types may not be fully developed, certain patterns may emerge that give us glimpses into their dominant traits. If we are observant, we can typically see kids moving in patterns that are common for their Harmony Triad and begin to help them integrate all three centers of intelligence.

By observing their behaviors, motivations, and ways of engaging with the world, we can start to identify their tendencies and support them from a harmonious perspective. This is our tool to assist us in parenting and not something we even need to reveal to our kids. We're not going to say, for example, "You're a Type 4, so of course you feel that way." Rather, you are going to keep this knowledge in your secret arsenal of parenting tools. It is your "Driver's Manual" that you will refer to as you seek to move your child along their path, parenting with intention and determination to guide them well so they can keep more of who they already are. Your job is to keep in mind those 3 informants. When a child is expressing deep emotion, for example, you are going to honor their feeling heart but also invite them to engage their body and do something (perhaps go for a walk together), and their thinking head to solve problems with other ideas or storylines.

As we think about the practical use of becoming Enneagram-informed, it is important to approach this conversation with wonder and openness, allowing room for growth and adaptability over time as your child matures.

Recognizing Strengths and Challenges in Each Center

Understanding the "Butterflies and Dragons" associated with each center of intelligence helps us tailor our support to our children's individual needs. With this acknowledgment, we can provide encouragement in areas of giftedness and offer support and guidance when the dragons arrive. I am going to give you specific examples and strategies for each type a little later, but for now, let me introduce the ways children will need support when they are operating from each of the centers.

- **Body Center: (Types 8, 9, & 1)** Children rooted in the body center tend to be action-oriented, instinctual, and practical. They will be enticed by the "Dragon of Anger" in different ways: Type 8s will be outwardly aggressive with their anger, while Type 9s will be more passive aggressive and Type 1s will turn their anger inward. They will each need caregivers to encourage their physical well-being, assertiveness, and groundedness while helping them balance their need for control and perfectionism.

- **Heart Center: (Types 2, 3, & 4)** Children with a strong connection to the heart center are often empathetic, compassionate, and relationally oriented. "Shame" is the name of the dragon these children will face. Type 2s will attempt to manage shame by caring for others, while Type 3s will seek to set feelings aside and manage shame through performance, and Type 4s may get lost in shame altogether. They will each need caregivers to nurture their emotional intelligence, helping them navigate their own emotions while also supporting their self-care, boundaries, and assertiveness.

- **Head Center: (Types 5, 6, & 7)** Children who gravitate towards the head center often possess strong analytical and problem-solving abilities. Each type in this center will be visited by the "Dragon of Fear." Type 5s may withdraw as they seek to conserve their energy, Type 6s may become dutiful as they seek to manage anxious thoughts, and Type 7s may act assertively as they seek security. They each will need caregivers to encourage their curiosity and critical thinking skills while also helping them manage tendencies towards overthinking and anxiety.

Balancing and Integrating the Centers Supporting the three centers of intelligence involves nurturing a sense of balance and integration among them. Again, this material will make more sense as you go along. Be patient and just absorb what you are learning before you attempt to apply it.

I am going to give you practical ways to interact with your child as you become an "Enneagram-informed" parent or caregiver. Teaching these concepts to our children from a young age is giving them the reins to be the masterful dragon tamer, orchestrating the flight of these powerful creatures. As they learn to harness the strength of their mind, the compassion of their heart, and the instinct of their gut, they become the fearless leaders of their own life's journey, taming their dragons with skill and grace.

Balancing and Integrating the Centers

As you become more familiar with the Enneagram and are mindfully present with your children, I believe you will begin to identify when your child is acting from one of their 3 centers of intelligence, if not their emerging Enneagram type. It is my hope that you will also begin to recognize your own type and its harmony counter types so that you can begin to develop greater awareness of your needs with self-compassion and intention.

Supporting the three centers of intelligence involves nurturing a sense of balance and integration among them. Teaching this concept to our children from a young age is like giving them the reins to be the masterful dragon tamer, orchestrating the flight of these powerful creatures. As they learn to harness the strength of their mind, the compassion of their heart, and the instinct of their gut, they become the fearless leaders of their own life's journey, taming their dragons with skill and grace.

I want to invite you to consider encouraging activities and practices that promote the integration of the three centers, such as:

Mind-Body Connection: Practices like yoga, meditation, or mindful movement help your child connect their physical sensations with their thoughts and emotions. This supports a holistic understanding of themselves and promotes a sense of inner harmony.

Creative Expression: Encourage your child to engage in artistic or expressive activities that tap into their emotions and physicality. Drawing, dancing, or playing an instrument can help integrate their centers while supporting self-expression.

Reflective Practices: Set aside dedicated time for your child to reflect on their thoughts, emotions, and bodily sensations through journaling, tracking, or open conversation with you. I like using "High, Low, Buffalo" - What was good, challenging, and surprising about your day?"

Why It Matters–Becoming Enneagram Informed

Yes, I'm going to say it again. In all my experiences and training as a Child and Family Therapist, my study and use of the Enneagram has been most enlightening. As an Attachment Therapist, it makes perfect sense when we consider how mindset is formed. As parents and caregivers, incorporating the Enneagram into our understanding of our children can deepen our connection and support their growth. It can shape how we communicate and guide our kids as we respect their unique qualities and needs.

There is no "one perfect way" to parent or lead kids. The Enneagram reveals that each of us has our own strengths and challenges, as do our children. By embracing this journey, you will have a roadmap for your own growth and self-development. It will shine a light on your own dragon, allowing you to be more aware of your core motivations and ego messages. With this awareness, I believe you will have greater compassion and understanding for yourself and the children in your life.

As over half of my clients have been kids between the ages of 6–12, I can't help wanting to point out the trends I have witnessed as a kind of secret key that has the potential to unlock so much clarity for parents and caregivers. I want to invite you to consider using this tool to bring your strategies into focus. You don't need to be concerned with "typing your child" and getting it just right. What matters more is developing a means to approach parenting with love and wonder, attuning to your child as you notice patterns, and adjusting your guidance.

The greatest thing you can do for your child is to do the work for yourself first. When you first understand how to show up for yourself, then and ONLY then can you raise your child well and become the parent they need. There is a process to personal growth, and once you understand it, your impact is limitless. This is why I am shifting my practice to training parents and caregivers. Together, we can raise caring and wholehearted kids.

Let's dive in. Not only will you learn about the types from a parent and child perspective, but I will share with you my TRUE parenting approach for each. Remember, parenting from this approach teaches Trust, Resilience, Uniqueness, and Empathy.

Friend, I want to remind you that children develop their Enneagram type with a sense of fluidity. I want to invite you to first read through this material with consideration to your own childhood experience. Make space to honor your experience or lack of support in any area. Then, shift your focus to leading the children in your life.

THE BODY CENTER TYPES:

8-9-1

CHAPTER 6

Eights

Meet Stephanie

Stephanie was just 9 when she was referred to me by her parents who seemed to be at their wit's end. Adopted at 3, Stephanie had known extreme neglect and hunger. She was having difficulty at school making and keeping friends due to her strong need to be in charge. Kids labeled her "bossy" and avoided her and her domineering energy on the playground. Play dates were often a disaster as she had to "be in charge" resulting in her guest wanting to go home early.

Type 8: "The Challenger" (Body Center)

When healthy, 8s are self-confident, strong, protective, resourceful, and decisive. They can seem to have an energy about them that is larger than life. Type 8s often use their strength to improve the lives of others, becoming noble and even heroic. They have a drive to feel powerful and in control, and being weak 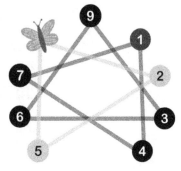 or vulnerable is avoided at all costs. 8s prefer respect over approval. Healthy 8s provide empathetic leadership and warm direction and can be vulnerable in relationships.

As Children

Children with an emerging Type 8 personality show assertiveness early on. Parents often report they are tough to raise as they have a high need for control and can be  combative. When struggling with their Dragon of Anger, an emerging Type 8 child may become overly confrontational and domineering, seeking to overpower others as a way to maintain their sense of strength and control.

Type 8 children, especially girls, will most likely get negative feedback from friends and may be rejected and called names by peers who want some power of their own. Often, they are labeled as "diffi-cult and obstinate" by teachers who don't always appreciate that they speak their mind. Parents will need to be sensitive while helping their child navigate this type of feedback and not be quick to say, "Well, if you weren't so bossy, they would maybe play with you more," which insults the very core of the 8 child. Instead, parents need to point out that their child has gifts that just need to be shaped. For exam-ple, parents can explain that leadership is a strength that carries a lot of responsibility, reminding them that good leaders care about the needs and feelings of others.

At Their Core

At their core, an 8 wants to be in control and move in their strength. Their "Dragon of Anger" tells them they need to be doing something and often shouts, "Ready, Fire, Aim!" The "Dragon of Anger" produces a flame that lights a sense of passion and urgency to push and move things forward. They struggle with its messages that tell them they need to make it happen and that they haven't done enough. They hear it say, "Don't trust anyone and stay strong and in control."

Signs of Their Dragon

You will know when 8s are battling their dragon as they will begin to appear overly controlling, arrogant, mean, insensitive, and confrontational. They may even become forceful, rageful bullies when they or their loved ones are threatened. They may struggle to allow themselves to trust or be close to others. They may be prone to excess with a "more is always better" attitude. If they let the dragon move in, 8s will be proud and bossy, calling the shots, directing the cruise, right the wrongs, and always needing to have the LAST word. When they are stressed, the 8 may display Type 5 qualities and can be withholding, cynical, detached, and intense.

TRUE Parenting

TRUST–We want to help an emerging 8 child learn to trust all three centers of intelligence. As they are in the body center and will experience a "forward moving" energy, we will need to help them find ways to take their foot off the gas and make conscious choices. As parents, we can encourage true growth by guiding our emerging 8 children to shift to the strengths of Types 2 and 5 in their harmony triad. For example, when struggling with control and aggression, we can remind them to notice the feelings and needs of others (2) as well as use their thinking minds to generate the best course or solution (5).

RESILIENCE–Building resilience in a Type 8 must include caring for their heart space as 8s are quick to jump on "grit" as a means to push through the "hard places." We want to help them feel safe in exploring their tenderness and compassionate hearts and remind them that one of their gifts is a natural inclination to protect and care for others.

UNIQUENESS–The goal here is to help your emerging Type 8 child learn that they don't have to conform and be like someone else. They get to celebrate their main strength, courage, as they learn to integrate strengths from their other two centers. In their case, having a strong sense of what to do (8) can be tempered with connecting to the thoughts and feelings of others (2) and slowing down to consider options before taking action (5).

EMPATHY–Parents can help their emerging 8 children build empathy for themselves and others by taming their Dragon of Anger with the following messages:

- "It's okay to trust others."
- "You don't have to always be in control."
- "You can count on your heart to help you connect to yourself and others."
- "There are others who can help you."
- "You can let go and relax."

Helping them internalize and grow true to these messages will result in self-talk that sounds like:

- "I can be brave and trust others."
- "Vulnerability is a sign of strength."
- "I don't always have to be in control."
- "I can let my feeling heart guide me and connect with someone."
- "I can slow down before I act."

Discipline

Parenting a child with an emerging Type 8 personality will require that you manage your own fear and need for control. Often, parents tell me they worry that their child will never have friends because they are so bossy and that their child only listens to them when they get loud and scary. Making calm connections while finding ways to share power will be imperative to maintaining a healthy relationship.

When an emerging Type 8 child is displaying behavior that requires discipline it will be important for parents and caregivers to not "lock horns" with them. These children, like all children, need to know that they have loving adults who are in charge and in control. Stay calm. While your buttons may be pushed, you're only human after all, it is imperative that you maintain your self-control. Boundaries need to be firm and consistent. Follow-through is important and necessary.

That said, don't be quick to lay down a consequence while reacting. You can always say, "I'll get back to you," and think about what you want to happen. Emerging 8 kids need adults who are confident, loving, and secure in their role to help them build trust from a relaxed state. When their adults are unclear or wavering, they will feel the innate pull to take over and lead.

Don't ask for their permission, which will only confuse them about who is in charge. Instead of saying, "If you do this, then would you like to…? Or qualify statements with "Okay?" Try, "After you do this, we are going to …"

Predictable, clear, and steady reminds them that they don't need to be in charge. You've got that role. Look for ways to put them in control of things that don't really matter. Ask them, for example, "Would you like the blue or red cup?" Use their language to appeal to their gifts. For example, you might say, "I need you to be in charge of setting the table," or "I need you to protect the feelings of your sister and be kind."

As they get older and need to problem solve, ask them to touch base with their feeling heart (2) and get curious about what others might be thinking or feeling. Lead them to their thinking head (5) to slow down and contemplate or research different ways to go about things. You may want to begin your discipline with a gentle reminder that you love them before asking them to change something. Then you might say, "Please take a deep breath and get control of your body and mouth." You can let them know that you want to hear from them, and want to be heard, but can't do that when they are "amped" or "wound up." Give them the power to choose how to get calm first so that connection wins over chaos.

Best Butterfly Self (2-5-8)

When a child emerges as a Type 8 Butterfly, they beautifully display the colors of courage, leadership, protectiveness, resourcefulness, self-confidence, and decisiveness. When all three centers of intelligence are integrated, the 8 can also be found exhibiting the strengths of the 2 through displays of loving kindness and heart-centered connection. Think of Dr. Martin Luther King Jr., who was a courageous leader (8) who connected compassionately with his followers (2) and led with discerning wisdom (5).

Suggestions for Parenting an Emerging 8

Parenting a Type 8 child involves recognizing their innate tendencies toward assertiveness, independence, and a desire for control. Here are some suggestions to effectively nurture and support your emerging Type 8 child:

- **Confront Gently:** Begin tough conversations in a non confrontational way if possible. Reminding them that you are on the same side helps get them out of "battle mode" and lowers their defenses.

- **Acknowledge Their Independence:** Emerging Type 8 children value their independence and assertiveness. Acknowledge and celebrate their natural leadership qualities and their ability to take initiative. Encourage them to make age-appropriate decisions, share control when appropriate, and give them room to assert themselves.

- **Teach Empathy and Collaboration:** While Type 8 children may have a strong sense of self, it's essential to teach them empathy and the value of cooperation. Encourage them to consider others' perspectives and feelings and demonstrate that assertiveness can coexist with kindness and understanding.

- **Model Healthy Communication:** Demonstrate effective communication by openly expressing your thoughts and feelings while also listening to theirs. Encourage them to express themselves assertively yet respectfully, teaching them that assertiveness can lead to constructive dialogue.

- **Set Clear Boundaries:** Type 8 children may test boundaries, so it's crucial to set clear and consistent rules. Explain the reasons behind the rules, helping them understand the importance of respecting boundaries while still allowing room for autonomy.

- **Promote Emotional Awareness:** Type 8 children may not always express their emotions openly. Create a safe and non-judgmental space for them to share their feelings. Encourage them to identify and communicate their feelings, teaching them that it's safe to be vulnerable and express themselves honestly with you.

- **Teach Conflict Resolution:** Type 8 children's assertiveness can sometimes lead to conflicts. Teach them healthy conflict resolution skills, such as active listening, compromise, and finding win-win solutions. Help them understand that conflicts can be resolved without resorting to aggression.

- **Support Their Interests:** Encourage them to pursue activities and interests that align with their passions and strengths. Celebrate their determination and drive, helping them channel their energy into constructive endeavors.

- **Model Accountability:** Demonstrate accountability by taking responsibility for your actions and decisions. Show them that acknowledging mistakes and making amends is a sign of strength and integrity.
- **Balance Independence with Collaboration:** Help them balance their desire for independence with the benefits of collaboration. Encourage them to work with others when appropriate, emphasizing that teamwork can lead to even greater achievements.

Remember that emerging Type 8 children have a strong sense of agency and can become the best version of themselves when nurtured with respect and guidance. They have so much to offer, and when their 8 instincts are integrated with their thoughts and feelings, they will become the leaders we so desperately need.

CHAPTER 7

Nines

Meet Jade

Jade was a quiet 11-year-old girl when she started seeing me. The youngest in her family, her parents expressed concern as she seemed to be getting lost in the crowd of their growing family. Jade was often unsure of what she thought or felt, and her parents found her quite stubborn and indecisive when they tried to help.

Type 9: "The Peacemaker" (Body Center)

Type 9 Individuals are known for being laid back and accepting. They are typically trusting and stable, relaxed and supportive. Healthy 9s are non-judgmental and concerned with the good of all, often forgetting their own agenda to create shared results. They are adaptable, patient, compassionate, and supportive. They are engaged and use their energy to address conflict/peace issues. Integrated 9s are diplomatic, simply succeeding for the sake of others.

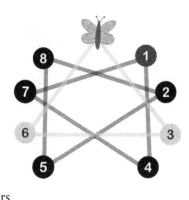

As a Child

Children with an emerging Type 9 personality are typically easygoing and kind-hearted. They have a strong desire for inner peace and harmony in their relationships and environment. These children are motivated by the need for peace and avoidance of conflict. When struggling with their dragon of anger, an emerging Type 9 child may become overly complacent and passive, avoiding confrontation and their own desires in favor of keeping the peace.

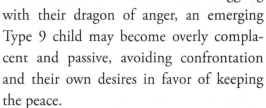

Type 9 children are typically well-liked as they are extremely compliant and go with the flow. My husband, who I met in the fourth grade, is a Type 9. He was so well-liked that two of our former classmates named their children after him. As parents, you may have concerns that your emerging Type 9 child tends to be a little too passive, finding yourself worrying that your child will be taken advantage of by peers. Parents often report that they have a tendency to get frustrated when their child answers, "I don't know," when asked their opinion. These parents wish their child would find their voice and state their opinions more readily. These children will need to be met with patience and given space to discern their thoughts and feelings in their own time.

At Their Core

At the core of a Type 9 is the desire to have peace of mind. They value inner harmony, and their biggest fear is loss of connection, mainly with themselves and their state of peace. Like 3s, 9s are in the middle of their center and can, at times, be disconnected from their needs, feelings, and anger as they adapt to support the agenda of others.

Type 9's face messages from the dragon of anger that sound like, "Your opinion doesn't matter as much as theirs," "Keep your head down," "Just keep the peace," and "Let them have what they want."

Signs of Their Dragon

You will know a Type 9 is being overwhelmed by their dragon when they appear indecisive, spaced-out, or avoidant. In this space, they can appear stuck and somewhat lost about what they need, feel, or want. They may procrastinate and find it difficult to take action. 9s may also engage in numbing behaviors or seek distractions such as over-eating, excessive sleeping, or binge-watching T.V. Their anger may come out in passive-aggressive behavior in the form of sarcasm and/or stubborn behavior. When stressed, 9s may display qualities of Type 6, becoming more focused on potential problems and risks to their sense of peace.

TRUE Parenting

TRUST–We want to help emerging Type 9 children learn to trust their instincts as well as their other two centers of intelligence: their feeling heart and thinking head. As they are in the body center, they wrestle with the Dragon of Anger but from a withdrawing stance. We will need to help them find ways to get off the sidelines and move into action, as 9s often know what to do but think someone else should do it. As parents, we can encourage true growth by guiding our emerging 9 children to shift to their Types 3 and 6 in the harmony triad. For example, when struggling with inaction or passive-aggressive anger, we can remind them to notice their own feelings (3) as well as use their thinking mind to generate the best course or solution (6).

RESILIENCE–Building resilience in a Type 9 must include finding ways to help our kids get present, recognize, and care for all three centers. Type 9s tend to push their anger down, and, like a beach ball held underwater, it can wildly pop out with great surprise to all. We want to help them stay awake to what they feel and give them opportunities to diffuse tension as they try to keep the peace at all costs. When they flare in anger, we will need to help them attend to the damage by making amends that include their acknowledgment of feelings while promoting self-compassion and understanding of their own humanity.

UNIQUENESS–The goal here is to help your emerging 9 children learn that they are amazing just as they are and that their thoughts and feelings matter. Remember, they value inner peace and harmony, but we need to teach them that they can manage discomfort and that sharing their thoughts and asking for what they need is valued. It will be important for the adults in their lives to notice when they are fading into the background or beginning to show stress under the surface. We want to look for "tells" that they are stressed and moving toward protecting their inner peace by "checking out" (my husband whistles) so that we can invite them to show up and connect.

EMPATHY–Type 9s need to be reminded that their presence matters. As parents and caregivers, we can encourage our emerging 9 children to assert themselves and offer them easy ways to practice making choices and finding their voice to express their needs and wants. At times, it may be easier for them to know what they *don't* want, and we phrase our questions to help them. For example, we might say, "Of these three options, which would you like the least?"

We want to combat their dragon with reassurance as we say, "You make a difference, and you matter to this family." Parents can help their emerging 9 children build empathy for themselves and others by taming their Dragon of Anger with the following messages:

- "It's okay to have your own opinion"
- "You don't have to comply with the wishes of others to keep the peace."
- "You can trust your instincts."
- "You can show up fully in life."
- "Your thoughts and feelings count, so check in and let me know."

You can guide them to internalize these messages with self-talk that sounds like:

- "My thoughts and feelings matter."
- "I can take my time to check in with all parts of myself."
- "I don't always have to be the peacemaker."
- "I can acknowledge my feelings and honor my needs."
- "I am human and doing my best."

Discipline

Parenting a child with an emerging Type 9 personality will require that you manage your own tendency to overly applaud their compliance. Often, parents tell me that their Type 9 child is easy and enjoyable but that they worry more may be going on inside. Asking your child to share their opinion, anger, and thoughts may seem like an unnecessary invitation to potential discord, but, in the long run, this intentional probing will help your child grow in greater balance and wellness.

When an emerging Type 9 child is displaying behavior that requires discipline, it may often be because they failed to take action on something you asked them to do. It may also stem from a burst of anger that takes everyone, including them, by surprise. It's important for Type 9 children to have loving adults that normalize their humanity and give them ways to fully experience their feelings. They will also need permission to seek balance and inner harmony, and you might encourage them to use their words to not only ask for what they want but also to acknowledge why. For example, while at a family function that may be busy and chaotic, your child may need to remove themselves. Teach them to say what they feel or think and ask for what they need. It might sound like, "I'm feeling overwhelmed by all the noise. I think I need to go outside."

Emerging 9 kids need adults who are patient with them and who will stretch them a bit from their comfort zone. When asking them for opinions as you try to include them more, it may be helpful to limit their choices. For example, you may say, "It's your turn to choose where we are going to eat. Here are three restaurants you can choose from." Or, "On a scale of 1-10, how do you feel about...?" Finding ways to help them touch base with themselves and find their voice is the goal of creating greater balance and integrating their centers.

It will be important that we help them develop a relationship with their body with strategies for maintaining their sense of peace and harmony. We can help them integrate their other two centers of intelligence, feeling heart and thinking head, by guiding them to shift to their butterfly strengths of 3 and 6. We can help them find ways to set goals and be effective (3) and to plan ahead for what they might need (6).

Best Butterfly Self (3-6-9)

When a child emerges as a Type 9 Butterfly, they beautifully display the colors of harmony, peacefulness, and serenity. They are calm and balanced, offering comfort and stability to others. When all three centers of intelligence are integrated, the 9 can also be found exhibiting the butterfly brilliance of the integrated triad 3-6-9. Think Abraham Lincoln, who has been labeled a Type 9 and who was known for his honesty and trustworthiness. A well-integrated Type 9 child can grow true to their life's calling working in a peaceful manner that makes others feel safe (9), is effective and inspiring (3), and with the ability to figure out the best way to improve situations for others (6).

Suggestions for Parenting an Emerging 9

Parenting a Type 9 child involves recognizing their innate tendencies towards kindness, harmony, and a strong need for peace. Here are some suggestions to effectively nurture and support your emerging Type 9 child:

- **Create a Peaceful Environment:** Foster a calm and harmonious home environment. Avoid unnecessary conflicts or tension, as Type 9 children are sensitive to discord. Guide them in developing healthy conflict-resolution skills. Teach them that addressing conflicts can lead to greater understanding and harmony in relationships.

- **Listen Actively & Be Patient:** Be a patient and attentive listener when your child wants to express their thoughts or feelings. Encourage them to share their opinions, knowing that their voice is valued. Type 9 children may take their time to make decisions or take action. Be patient and supportive as they navigate choices and changes in their lives.

- **Respect Their Need for Space:** Type 9 children may occasionally withdraw to avoid conflict or stress. Respect their need for solitude and personal space and let them know it's okay to take breaks when they need to recharge.

- **Set Clear Expectations:** Provide clear and reasonable expectations and boundaries. This helps them feel secure and know what is expected of them.

- **Foster Independence & Expression:** While Type 9 children may prioritize peace and cooperation, encourage them to develop their individual interests and goals. Help them find their own passions and ambitions. Help them overcome overwhelm by offering them options to choose from. Support their self-expression through creative activities such as art, music, or journaling. These outlets can help them explore their feelings and thoughts.

- **Promote Physical Activity:** Encourage physical activities or sports that help them stay connected with their bodies and energy levels. This can help prevent them from becoming too passive or complacent.

- **Celebrate Their Efforts:** Recognize and celebrate their accomplishments and efforts, even the small ones. This encourages them to stay engaged and motivated. Remind them that their presence and contribution make a difference.

- **Model Healthy Assertiveness:** Demonstrate healthy assertiveness and teach them that it's okay to express their needs and desires without fear of conflict. Show them that assertiveness can lead to positive outcomes.

By providing a supportive, harmonious atmosphere, respecting their need for space, and teaching healthy communication and conflict-resolution skills, you can help Type 9 children emerge as balanced, peaceful individuals who can effectively navigate life's challenges while offering their gift of stability and calmness to the world.

CHAPTER 8

Ones

Meet Casey

Casey was 8 when she came to counseling as her parents began to notice symptoms of anxiety and stress. They had no complaints about her behavior and said she was frequently "hard on herself." She often got frustrated while doing homework and shut down. When she first came to see me, I noticed that she immediately used words like "right" and "wrong" when describing how to do life. When she started to share more, she stated that she was afraid she was "a bad person."

Type 1: "The Improver" (Body Center)

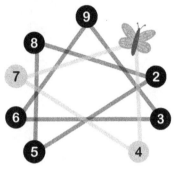

Type 1s are known for being self-disciplined, hardworking, organized, and discerning. They can be noble, conscientious as well as morally heroic. Healthy 1s are principled and can reform what is wrong and make it right. They are ethical and trustworthy and motivated by the need to live life well, including making themselves and the things around them better.

As a Child

Children with an emerging Type 1 personality strive for perfection and have a strong sense of right and wrong. They are motivated by the desire to improve themselves and their world. They are conscientious and responsible and ready to follow the rules or break them if it is for the higher good. They may be proud of their performance at school, with a tendency to set high expectations for themselves and others.

Emerging Type 1 children want to be good. They want to get it right and may have an unreasonable belief that being wrong or doing wrong equals being a bad person. For many of them, falling short of perfection is the same as failure. In this mindset, a grade below A may as well be an F. The biggest bully your child will face is the one living inside their own head. This critic is active and loud and tells the Type 1 that they need to do more and do it really well in order to be accepted and loved.

Parents will need to be careful not to praise their performance or label their behavior as good or bad to the extent that it feeds their Dragon of Anger that is sensitive to the way things "should be" at all times. Instead, parents need to balance their praise with applause for taking risks and making mistakes, being messy and playful, and releasing the outcome of things in exchange for the joy of being in the moment. An example of this practice might be inviting our emerging 1 child to use watercolor paint with us, just for the fun of it, with the thought of throwing it away when we're done.

At Their Core

At their core, a Type 1 wants to be good and moral and wrestles with imperfection. In the Body Center, 1s battle the Dragon of Anger that partners with a critic that often directs its anger inward. Together, they shout messages to the emerging Type 1 child that say: "Fix it." "Make it better." "It's hopeless." "You're not good enough." "You need to improve." They may even hurl hurtful messages when mistakes are made, like: "You're so stupid!" "What is wrong with you?" "No one is going to love you like this."

Signs of Their Dragon

You will know when 1s are being bullied by their dragon as they will begin to exhibit heightened anxiety and a strong need for control and orderliness. Their inner critic demands another tweak or correction to make things perfect. On their edge, 1s have repressed anger and can be picky, self-righteous, judgmental, and impatient. They can be hypercritical of themselves and others, rigid, inflexible, and controlling. They may become heartbroken and sad in a world that seems unjust and lacks integrity. In this space, an emerging 1 child may even seem to "lose it" over something minor like a homework problem. And though they may seem they're throwing a fit on the outside, a closer look will reveal a child crumbling on the inside.

TRUE Parenting

TRUST–Emerging Type 1 children will need us to help them trust all three centers of intelligence. Also, from the body center, these kids battle the Dragon of Anger that strategizes in cooperation with their "inner bully." Type 1s will take a dependent stance, moving toward others with a fierce determination to seek their approval. We will need to teach them how to calm their dragon and inner bully by helping them reframe their messages to be more patient and compassionate.

Recently, I worked with a child who was asking if she could be "un-adopted" if she was bad. We were building her life book together with her mom, who shared that this question comes up a lot no matter how many times she has tried to reassure her daughter, who she adopted at

2 months old. I had her daughter look at a photo of the day she came home to her family. I said, "Your parents adopted a tiny human who they knew, because she was human, wasn't perfect." I continued sharing through loving but intense eye contact, saying, "Honey, you aren't perfect and can never be perfect." She looked worried.

I continued, "You will make mistakes, but that doesn't make you bad...it makes you human. You can never be perfect, but you will always be loved because you are worthy, just as you are...and that will never change." She gave a big sigh of relief as her mom smiled at her in support of my words and sentiment. Recognizing her daughter as an emerging Type 1 and adopted, her mom knows that she will need to hear this message many more times.

RESILIENCE–Building resilience in an emerging Type 1 will require that we assist them in reshaping their ideal with a more "human-friendly" expectation of themselves and others. They need us to remind them that they are loved for who they are, "warts and all," which will require that we are mindful to be loving when they make mistakes or don't quite hit the mark. They will need our guidance toward their harmony strengths of Types 4 and 7. We can invite them to lay down their perfectionistic intensity to notice the beauty in the world around them (4) and experience childlike wonder and joy (7).

UNIQUENESS–The goal here is to help your emerging 1 child learn that they get to celebrate their way of living in the world with standards, diligence, and attention to justice, as well as learning to hold compassion and grace for themselves and others. In their case, having a strong sense of right and wrong (1) can be tempered with playful innocence (7) and creative expression and exploration of all emotions (4).

EMPATHY–Parents can help their emerging 1 child build empathy for themselves and others by taming their Dragon of Anger with the following truths:

- "Mistakes are how we learn."
- "No one is perfect."
- "It's good to also relax and play."
- "It's important to take care of our feelings."

You can guide them to internalize these messages to result in self-talk that sounds like:

- "I am only human."
- "I am doing my best."
- "I can focus on my part and recognize I am only one person."
- "I can find my voice to inspire others to action."

Discipline

Parenting a child with an emerging Type 1 personality can be challenging. I often hear parents say they are at a loss because their child is already so hard on themselves. They express that they don't want to discipline their child because it appears that she is already on the edge. But discipline, in the real sense of the word, is what an emerging Type 1 needs.

Especially in the case of parenting an emerging Type 1 child, discipline needs to look like training. It's guidance that teaches proper balance, making repairs, and acknowledging one's mistakes. Type 1s need to learn that the world isn't going to fall apart and that they aren't bad, defective, or unlovable when they have misbehaved. Instead, we can show them how to course correct and move on. Whew! What a relief.

When a Type 1 child escalates, normally in frustration that things aren't working quite as planned around homework, cooking, or a special project, it will be important that you direct them to move their energy out of their body in a healthy way, and then come back and try again. There can be a level of intensity for improvement that 1s experience, and often they can "lock in" on whatever it is that they are trying to perfect. At times, it will appear that a Type 1 is going to self-combust, and we want to help them notice and care for themselves before that, or an explosion toward others, happens. In a loving but firm way, you can direct them by saying, "I need you to take a break for 15 minutes while you go outside for a walk/run and then come back."

As they get older, 1s will need to be able to manage their intense need to make all things right, good, and perfect, finding ways to strike a balance as they move through life. Lead them to their feeling heart (4) and thinking head (7) to help them relax and enjoy their life in the present moment. Help them develop self-care strategies as a regular practice and praise their ability to accept themselves and others just as they are.

Best Butterfly Self (1-4-7)

When a healthy child emerges as a Type 1 Butterfly, they will radiate the colors of responsibility, morality, justice, diligence, fairness, and principled dependability. Type 1s need to remember that they are innately worthy of love and belonging. As parents, we can encourage balance by guiding our child to integrate their three centers according to their 1-4-7 harmony triad. Think Greta Thunberg, the Swedish environmental activist who, at age 15, became brokenhearted at the world's climate change crisis and the irresponsible acts of so many (1) who adventurously campaigned with a school walkout (7) and passionately challenged world leaders with heartfelt speeches (4) to take action.

Suggestions for Parenting an Emerging 1

Parenting a Type 1 child requires understanding their natural inclination for order, responsibility, and adherence to rules as well as the role of their inner critic. Here are some suggestions to create a nurturing environment for a Type 1 child to emerge as their best butterfly self.

- **Provide Clear Expectations and Structure:** Establish clear boundaries, rules, and routines to create a structured environment. Clearly communicate your expectations and the reasoning behind rules to help your child understand their importance.

- **Encourage Flexibility:** Teach your child that making mistakes is a part of learning and growth. Encourage flexibility and self-compassion, emphasizing the importance of effort and progress over perfection. Encourage them to set realistic expectations for themselves and others.

- **Model and Encourage Emotional Expression:** Create a safe space for your child to express their feelings openly. Encourage them to label and communicate their emotions and ask for what they need. Teach them healthy ways to manage stress and frustration.

- **Promote Ethical Values:** Engage in discussions about fairness, honesty, and justice. Encourage your child to speak up when they witness injustice and guide them in understanding complex moral issues.

- **Support Self-Worth:** If your child is prone to self-criticism, teach them that they are inherently valuable regardless of their achievements. Emphasize self-acceptance and the importance of treating themselves with kindness and understanding.

- **Celebrate Effort and Progress:** Acknowledge and celebrate your child's hard work and progress toward their goals, regardless of the outcome. This reinforces the value of determination and personal growth.

- **Encourage Responsibility:** Assign age-appropriate responsibilities to help your child develop a sense of accountability and competence. Praise their reliability and trustworthiness.

- **Promote Critical Thinking:** Encourage your child to think critically and evaluate situations based on facts and evidence. Teach them the importance of making informed decisions.

- **Provide a Structured Routine:** Establish a consistent daily routine that allows your child to plan and organize their activities. This helps them feel secure and prepared for daily tasks.

- **Model Integrity:** Be a role model for honesty, integrity, and ethical behavior. Show your child the importance of doing what is right, even when it's challenging.

- **Encourage Curiosity:** While Type 1 children may prioritize order and responsibility, encourage their natural curiosity and creativity. Provide opportunities for exploration and learning in various areas of interest.

By implementing these strategies, you can help your Type 1 child thrive and develop their unique strengths so that they emerge with a healthy balance and sense of self, knowing they are inherently good just as they are.

THE HEART CENTER TYPES:

2-3-4

CHAPTER 9

Twos

Meet Ella

Ella is a sweet 9-year-old who was referred to me by her parents, who were concerned that she was being taken advantage of by friends. It seemed that in order to win people over to herself, Ella was happy to give away things of value, like her own toys and even money from Mom's purse. When asked, she simply said, "I wanted to help them and make them happy, so they would like me."

Type 2: "The Helper" (Heart Center)

A Type 2 is the friend everyone wants. They are helpful, nurturing, sincere, and warmhearted. Generous, friendly, and self-sacrificing, 2s have strong interpersonal skills and

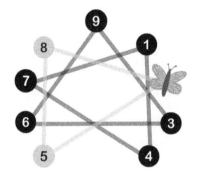

naturally give their attention to the needs of others. Healthy 2s can love others well while respecting their own needs and boundaries.

As a Child

Children with an emerging Type 2 personality are naturally empathetic and caring. They have an innate desire to help and support those around them. These children often put others' needs before their own and are motivated by a deep desire for love and acceptance. When struggling with their Dragon of Shame, a child with an emerging Type 2 personality may become overly accommodating, neglecting their own needs and desperately seeking validation through their acts of love and helpfulness.

Children exhibiting Type 2 behavior are generally so loving and kind that they are well-liked by peers and teachers. Parents may often refer to them as "Mommy's (or Daddy's) little helper," and they learn from an early age that this quality gets them lots of attention and positive feedback. You may find yourself worrying about your emerging 2 children as you notice that they sacrifice to meet the wishes of others. It's not uncommon for a parent to gasp as their child gives away a beloved toy to another child just because "they liked it." It may seem that they even use flattery, which can become manipulative, to get positive feedback and attention.

Emerging Type 2 children need adults in their lives to appreciate their love and care for others while also pointing out that they, too, have feelings and needs that are valid. They will need support to understand the difference between boundaries and selfishness, as it will be counterintuitive for a 2 to say "no" from a place of concern for potentially hurting someone's feelings.

At Their Core

Type 2s at their core have a desire to be loved and fear that they will be unloved or rejected. Their Dragon of Shame asserts messages such as: "You are unwanted," "You will be rejected if..." and "You might lose their love if you don't..." It tells them to use their gifts of discerning the needs of others and displaying loving kindness as a means to ensure that they are not rejected. Their gifts become tools to combat shame instead of natural expressions of who they were created to be in the world.

Signs of Their Dragon

When 2s are losing the battle with their dragon, they can appear clingy, manipulative, people-pleasing, co-dependent, and prideful. They will seem desperate to have the approval of others. They can work beyond their boundaries and those they are trying to care for. When influenced by their dragon, 2s are proud of their giving and can be boastful and resentful. At times, they may become addicted to loving and proving nobody can love you like they can. In this space, no good deed goes uncounted, and they can become martyr-like. When they are not integrating their head-heart-body intelligences, they may even display some of the 8s Dragon of Anger traits and become controlling and aggressive in their stress.

TRUE Parenting

TRUST–You can help your emerging 2 child tame their Dragon of Shame by reminding them that they are safe in connection with you as you help them trust their head and body intelligence along with their heart. In stress they will take a dependent stance and find it very difficult to not be overly concerned with the expectations and needs of others.

As parents and caregivers, we can encourage them to shift to their harmony strengths of Types 5 and 8. For example, when struggling with patterns of flattery and "over-giving," we can invite them to use wise thinking (5) as well as the courage to ask for what they need (8).

RESILIENCE–Building resilience in a Type 2 will require an intention to "think things through" instead of getting caught in the cycle of feeling and doing. It may be hard for a Type 2 to resist being the "helper," and important to point out when helping is healthy. For example, you may gently illustrate that helping may actually be seen as a form of control if it hasn't been asked for. We want to teach our children to respect others and allow them space to say or ask for what they need and help our 2's honor the right of others to struggle or do things on their own, which provides opportunities for people to grow and get stronger.

UNIQUENESS–The goal here is to help your emerging 2 child learn that they don't have to always help, enable, or rescue others; they get to celebrate their loving nature as they learn to integrate strengths from their other two centers. In their case, having a strong sense of what someone needs (2) can be tempered with connecting to thinking wisely (5) and taking courageous action (8).

EMPATHY–Parents can help their emerging 2 child build empathy for themselves by taming their Dragon of Shame with the following messages:

- "You don't have to earn love."
- "It's okay to have your own needs and feelings, and I am here to help you."
- "You can invite your thinking head to help you decide."
- "Let your heart take a moment to help you know what YOU feel."
- "You are loved unconditionally."

Ultimately, you want to teach them to internalize these messages as automatic responses to their dragon. They may sound like:

- "I'm okay. I am loved for who I am, not what I do."

- "I can have my own needs and feelings."
- "I can ask for what I need and receive help from others."
- "I need to take a deep breath and check in with my thinking head."
- "I can say no and still be lovable."

Discipline

Parenting a child with an emerging Type 2 personality will require that you balance your own patterns of reinforcing their "helper" behavior. Often, parents tell me they worry that their child will be vulnerable at school as they seem so sensitive and easy to hurt. Helping your child feel securely connected with the adults in their life will help lessen their fear of rejection. Look for ways to reinforce your bond with them, especially when it is totally unrelated to their acts of giving. For example, just catch them a moment after play and say, "I sure love you, even when you are sweaty and dirty."

When an emerging Type 2 child is displaying behavior that requires discipline it will be important for parents and caregivers to be mindful to separate their behavior from their worth. With all kids, we want to say, "I'm unhappy with your choice to …" and not, "You make me so crazy mad!" But with our Type 2 kids, we have to be extra careful. We want to calmly address their behavior in a way that is sandwiched between statements of love and empathy. It might sound like, "I love you, and that will never change. I need to remind you that your choice to … has resulted in a consequence of … and that makes me really sad. I don't like to see someone I love put themselves in this position."

Remember, you are showing your emerging Type 2 child how boundaries and follow-through can look in a relationship, so the discipline you use should be firm but loving. If your emerging 2, is under a lot of stress, they may act out in a way that reflects their type 8 tendencies. In this case, remain calm and protect your relationship by managing your own anger. You might say, "I understand that you are angry, but I need you to give me words I can understand and try that again with respect."

As they grow, you can guide them to engage their "thinking head" center before acting on their desire to meet the needs of others. Encourage them to ask themselves, "Am I doing something this person could do for herself?" "Does this person want my help?" "Can I give my help and care without expecting anything in return?"

Best Butterfly Self (2-5-8)

A healthy emerging 2 will wear the colors of loving-kindness, generosity, hospitality, servanthood, loving care, and empathy. They will do so without the intention of winning people's affection and admiration but just because it is who they are in their best self. When they are operating from this space and experiencing head-heart-body integration, they will also be able to access the strengths of type 4, heightening their appreciation for beauty, love, and creativity. In their 2-5-8 harmony, they will be world changers. Think Mr. Rogers. With gentleness and love (2) he thoughtfully wrote every show (5) and bravely took on important issues of his time (8).

Suggestions for Parenting an Emerging 2

Parenting a Type 2 child involves understanding their natural inclination to be caring and helpful in order to obtain the connection they crave. Here are some suggestions to effectively nurture and support the chrysalis of a Type 2 child:

- **Acknowledge and Appreciate Their Kindness:** Recognize and celebrate your child's natural inclination to help and care for others. Express your appreciation for their thoughtfulness and generosity, especially when done without expectation of recognition.

- **Teach Boundaries:** While Type 2 children love to help, it's important to teach them about setting healthy boundaries. Encourage them to express their own needs and emotions and help them find kind ways to say "no" when they need personal space or time for themselves.

- **Encourage Self-Care:** Help them understand the importance of self-care and self-love. Teach them that taking care of themselves is not selfish but essential for their well-being. Remind them that self-care is different from self-indulgence and healthy self-care helps sustain their ability to care for others and set a positive example.

- **Promote Independence:** While Type 2 children enjoy helping others, encourage them to develop their independence and self-reliance. Allow them to complete age-appropriate tasks on their own to help foster a sense of competence.
- **Validate Their Feelings:** Type 2 children may sometimes prioritize others' feelings over their own. Create a safe space for them to express their emotions openly and validate their experiences. Praise them for identifying and respecting their feelings in a healthy way.
- **Teach Assertiveness:** Empower them to assert themselves and communicate their needs and boundaries clearly. Help them find a balance between caring for others and advocating for themselves.
- **Promote Healthy Relationships:** Encourage them to build healthy, balanced relationships. Teach them about the importance of reciprocity and that relationships should be based on mutual care and respect.
- **Model Self-Compassion:** Demonstrate self-compassion by showing them that it's okay to make mistakes and prioritize self-care. Teach them to treat themselves with the same kindness and understanding they offer to others.
- **Celebrate Their Individuality:** Emphasize that their worth is not solely determined by how much they do for others. Celebrate their individuality

and unique qualities, helping them understand that they are valued just for being themselves.

- **Encourage Pursuit of Their Own Interests:** Support them in pursuing their own interests and passions, apart from caregiving. Help them explore hobbies and activities that bring them joy and fulfillment.

Remember that Type 2 children are naturally compassionate and caring, and it will be important for parents and teachers to not only encourage these qualities but also find other things to notice and praise. They need the adults in their lives to help them balance their loving nature with asserting themselves and using their thinking head in order for them to grow true to themselves and share their gifts in a healthy and balanced way.

CHAPTER 10

Threes

Meet Madison

Madison came to see me when she was just 9 years old. Her hair was curled, and she wore a sparkly T-shirt with "Girl Power" written in pink sequins. She was the type of child who seemed to have all the right answers and seemed eager to impress. When it came time to do an art project in our Kid's Group, she retreated to the tent in my office, embarrassed and afraid to share the words she had written reflecting her dragon's messages. When she finally did share with me privately, they told a completely different story than the one she had been selling through her projected confidence. It was one of insecurity and shame.

Type 3: "The Achiever" (Heart Center)

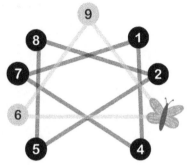

The song "Shiny Happy People" by REM comes to mind when I think of Type 3s. They are adaptable, achievement-oriented people who appear self-assured, competent, and energetic. They are often the ones who inspire us and who seem to have the world by its tail. 3s appear self-assured, energetic, confident and optimistic. Often, they grow up to be magnetic, ambitious, and energetic leaders who live up to their potential.

As a Child

Children with an emerging Type 3 personality are driven and performative. They have a strong desire to excel and be successful in whatever they undertake. These children are motivated by the need for achievement and recognition in order to feel valued. When struggling with their Dragon of Shame, an emerging Type 3 child may become overly concerned with their image, striving for perfection and sometimes sacrificing their truth to maintain their desired image of success.

Kids displaying traits of Type 3 will more than likely get some positive feedback, especially from the adults in their lives. Type 3s typically excel at something, if not many things. They are the "shining stars" of the class, the team, and the family. If they appear to have their stuff together, it's because they do.

Parents may worry that their emerging Type 3 child might shine a little too bright, drawing some negative attention from other kids who might assume they are arrogant, calling them "class pet" or "favorite child" in the home.

These children will need adults in their lives to recognize that, though they are in the heart center, they often don't acknowledge feelings in order to stay on course with whatever they are trying to accomplish. This may be the child who stays with a sport because they are good at it, despite the fact that they really don't enjoy it, or the child who pushes through an illness because there is a test at school. Parents will need to remember that their child displaying 3 traits often appears as if everything is great but may be denying what they really feel or need.

At Their Core

The core desire of a 3 is to be effective. They have a strong need to achieve and wrestle the Dragon of Shame that tells them their worth is tied to their accomplishments. In the middle of the Feeling Center, 3s have an uncanny ability to disregard feelings in order to get things done. They hear their dragon say: "You are a reflection of what you do." "Suck it up, Buttercup." "Push through." and "Prove you're worthy to be on the team."

Signs of Their Dragon

You will know 3s are being overwhelmed by their dragon when the cracks start to show. Sometimes, this looks like physical illness as their body attempts to get them to slow down. They may appear stressed and addicted to the need to be the best, most successful, and admired for whatever they are trying to do. When trapped by their dragon, they disconnect from their deeper feelings and lose touch with themselves and others. When on their edge, 3s may display the adaptive traits of Type 9, becoming more indecisive, complacent, or passive-aggressive.

TRUE Parenting

TRUST–We want to help the emerging 3 child learn to trust all three centers of intelligence. Type 3s have a stance in the world that is labeled "aggressive," meaning that they are most likely to be thinking of what's next with an energy that is independent and pushing forward. For our kids, this means that they may prioritize their goals over their well-being. We want to encourage them to invite their thinking head and sensing body to the party, as well as their feeling heart, as emerging 3s often choose to ignore feelings. Like 8s, these kids experience a "forward moving" posture toward life and will need help being in the present moment and mindfully pausing to check-in. As parents and leaders, we can encourage true growth by guiding them to shift to the high side of their harmony counterparts, Types 9 and 6. For example, we can encourage them to take a break and "just be" without action (9), as well as being faithful and compassionate to friends and teammates (6).

RESILIENCE–Building resilience in a Type 3 must include learning how to be more mindfully present and connected. 3s have a pattern of hyper-focusing on what needs to get done with an "eye on the prize," which can rob them of true presence. Mindfulness practices with these kids are extra beneficial to train them to slow down and connect.

UNIQUENESS–The goal here is to help your emerging 3 child learn that they don't have to perform to be loved, and they get to figure out who they really are and celebrate being that person. By honoring what they feel, they can have greater inner peace (9) and be genuinely more connected to others (6).

EMPATHY–Parents can encourage integration by guiding our emerging 3 children to shift to the butterfly strengths of Types 6 and 9. We have to be extra diligent to protect our 3s, as their dragon is indulged, especially in certain cultures. For example, when the world is telling them "great job" for over-performing, we can encourage them to shift to their thoughts and question what might go wrong for them if they don't acknowledge their needs (6) and make room for inner peace and quiet (9).

We need to remind them that they are loved and valued at all times, whether they win or lose. We want to encourage them by asking the following:

- "How are you really feeling?"
- "What do you need to take care of yourself?"
- "Let's slow down and just be together."
- "Just come as you are."

We want them to internalize our messages so that their adult self-talk includes:

- "I am not my job."
- "I don't need to impress anyone."
- "I am loved just as I am."
- "I know what I feel and what I need because I listen to my heart and body."
- "I don't need to do life with my hair on fire."
- "I can slow down and be present."

Discipline

It can be easy to allow them to be out of balance, pushing toward goals, when everyone loves a win. Parenting a child with an emerging Type 3 personality will require that you manage your own pride for having such a "shining star" as a son or daughter.

Often, parents tell me it's difficult to know when their emerging 3 child needs help until there is a "crash" of sorts. When discipline is necessary, these kids may have a hard time "being wrong". They may be prone to arguing and/or struggle with shame to have lost your admiration.

It will be important for parents and caregivers to remain calm and communicate clearly. Type 3s will thrive when you are able to clearly separate their behavior from their worth, so you will need to find a way to talk about what they did or didn't do and what you expect from them going forward. You will need to reassure them that they are loved and supported just as they are, normalizing that we all make mistakes, while you give them consequences and means to "make repair."

As with all heart-centered kids, we don't want to use words like, "You really disappointed me" or "I expected more from you," which feeds their Dragon of Shame and translates to these kids as "You just risked being disconnected from my love." Instead, we can say, "I will always love you, and consequences are just part of learning." "It makes me sad to tell you that you just lost your privilege for…." "You can make repair by …"

As they get older and need to problem solve, ask them to acknowledge and honor their feeling heart (3) and not just set feelings aside in order to get things done. Encourage them to also get curious about what might work best for everyone (6) and also practice letting go and just being present (9).

Best Butterfly Self (3-6-9)

When a child emerges as a Type 3 Butterfly, they beautifully display the colors of confidence, clarity, leadership, and productivity. They are often very organized, hard-working, and effective in providing inspiration to others. When fully integrated with their three centers of intelligence, they lead by example in a bold way. Think Oprah Winfrey, who is incredibly diverse in her pursuits and accomplishments. She has been called the most influential woman in the world (3) with a thirst for understanding and achieving deep inner peace (9) while giving consideration as to how to make the world a better place for all (6).

Suggestions for Parenting an Emerging 3

Parenting a Type 3 child involves recognizing their natural inclinations toward achievement, ambition, and a desire for success. Here are some suggestions to effectively nurture and support your emerging Type 3 child:

- **Acknowledge Their Achievements:** Recognize and celebrate your child's accomplishments, whether big or small. Offer praise and encouragement to boost their self-esteem and motivation, but be mindful to acknowledge their character traits over the outcome. Praise their willingness to make mistakes, take breaks, and respect their own feelings and needs.

- **Encourage Authenticity:** Teach your child that their worth is not solely defined by their achievements. Encourage them to embrace their true self and follow their passions and interests rather than pursuing success solely for external validation. Tell them, "You are loved for yourself. It's okay to have your own feelings and identity."

- **Promote a Healthy Balance:** Help your child strike a balance between pursuing their goals and enjoying life. Encourage them to engage in hobbies, relaxation, and spending quality time with family and friends. Notice and praise them for taking care of themselves as they find balance with fun and relaxation.

- **Teach Resilience:** Emphasize the importance of resilience and the ability to bounce back from setbacks. Teach them that failures are opportunities for growth and learning, not reasons to give up. Help them separate achievement from self-worth.

- **Model Healthy Competition:** Demonstrate sportsmanship and the importance of competing fairly and respectfully. Encourage them to enjoy the process of competing and the value of learning from both wins and losses. Emphasize the importance of integrity and ethical behavior. Teach them that success should be achieved with honesty and fairness.

- **Support Their Interests:** Encourage your child to explore and pursue activities and interests that align with their passions and strengths. Celebrate their determination and drive in these pursuits. Teach your child about the satisfaction of pursuing goals for the intrinsic joy of the process rather than solely for external rewards or recognition.

Remember, Type 3 children will often be celebrated and encouraged in their achievement-driven behavior. Help them remember to check in with their own feelings and needs and remind them that their worth and value are inherent in who they are and not what they do.

CHAPTER 11

Fours

Meet Julian

Julian was referred to me when he was 7 as he was having difficulty making friends. His parents reported that he often appeared sad and was "overly sensitive." As someone who was also labeled "overly sensitive," I couldn't wait to spend time with him. He loved my art supplies and wasn't afraid to go for it with the glitter. He came to life as he felt safe to express his creativity and shared at a profoundly deep level for his age. He explained that no one really liked him and that he was often made fun of at school.

Type 4: "The Creative" (The Heart Center)

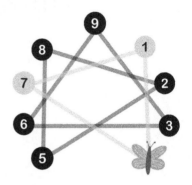

Type 4s are self-aware, sensitive, and offer beauty and creative energy. They are authentic and self-revealing, emotionally honest, and personal. Healthy 4s are not afraid to live in the beauty, celebration, tragedy, and grief of life. They are primarily motivated by the need to understand and express their deep feelings. They long to discover what is authentic in themselves and intentionally use their highly developed imagination, creativity, and inspiration to renew themselves and restore others. Integrated 4s allow the height and depth of their souls to be used as gifts to lead others to self-awareness.

As a Child

Children with an emerging Type 4 personality are introspective and emotionally attuned. They have a deep longing to be seen and understood for their uniqueness and value authenticity. Under stress, a child with a Type 4 personality may become emotionally reactive, withdrawn, and prone to mood swings. They may exhibit heightened sensitivity and a preoccupation with feelings of being misunderstood or unimportant. They may, at times, get stuck in melancholy and have mood swings.

It can be hard to be an emerging Type 4 child, as they are often told by others to "lighten up," "don't be so sensitive," and asked, "why are you such a baby?" Of course, these remarks only leave Type 4s with hurt feelings and a sense of being unloved and misunderstood. Cue the Dragon of Shame.

Parents have told me that they feel frustrated by their child's "thin skin" and feel held captive by their emotional reactions to almost everything they seem to do. They want to know how to "toughen them up" so they can face the "real" world.

At Their Core

At the core of a Type 4 is the desire to be understood. They are deeply afraid that their life may lack significance and long to be seen as unique and special. At times they can envy the contentment they believe others have and long for something that seems to be missing. In the heart center, 4s are known for deeply feeling their feelings and are motivated to understand and express them. 4s wrestle the Dragon of Shame, who tells them, "You're forgotten," "You're special and different, but no one cares," and "Stay in your dark feelings and go deeper into sadness."

Signs of Their Dragon

When 4s are facing their Dragon of Shame, they can be moody, self-absorbed, hypersensitive, intense, and melodramatic. In this space, they often feel misunderstood or shamed. When driven by the need to feel special, they can miss the joy found in everyday life. They can have problems with self-indulgence, hypersensitivity, worthlessness, and idealism, as well as depression and self-loathing. In this space, 4s can withhold themselves from others due to feeling vulnerable and defective or display traits of Type 2, becoming more emotionally needy and dependent on others. They may even become more people-pleasing and overly involved in the lives of others.

To live from their best self, 4s will need help developing equanimity, or the ability to have mental calmness and composure when things get stressful. As parents and caregivers, we can help them build equanimity as we remind them that feelings don't last forever.

We can begin by encouraging them to shift to their harmony strengths of their sensing body and thinking head, Types 1 and 7. For example, when struggling with feeling misunderstood, we can invite them to think optimistically and playfully engage (7), move their body, and *do* something like taking a walk in nature (1). 4s will need the adults in their lives to remind them, "You are seen for who you are." "It's okay to be happy." "Look for joy in the small, everyday moments."

TRUE Parenting

TRUST–We want to help the emerging Type 4 child learn to trust all three centers of intelligence. As they are in the heart center and will experience a "withdrawing" stance, we will need to help them find ways to disengage from the downward spiral of emotion by engaging their "doing center" or body.

As parents, we can encourage true growth by guiding our emerging 4 children to shift to the harmony strengths of Types 1 and 7. For example, when struggling with feelings of melancholy, we can remind them to playfully engage and consider gratitude (7) and move their body and do something (1).

RESILIENCE–Building resilience in an emerging Type 4 must include teaching them how to honor feelings without giving them too much power. These children will have an onslaught of invitations to experience emotions throughout their day. It will be crucial to teach them how to acknowledge them without fully embracing each one. Some, like a pushy salesperson, will need to stay beyond the fence, or our 4s will find them on their porch, in the front door, and setting up residency on the couch of their heart.

UNIQUENESS–The goal here is to help your emerging Type 4 child learn that they have a tenderness that is worth noting, but they also have the ability to do hard things. Emotions are their superpower when they are integrated with their sensing body (1) and thinking head (7). We will need to gently, and oh so carefully, honor their thoughts and feelings and then help them to let them go. We will need to do this in a way that is not dismissive or patronizing but sincere and reassuring. Our kids need to hear that they are "special and different, but not so special and different." They are people who are equipped to notice more beauty and pain, but they are also just people, humans, doing their best, like the rest of us.

EMPATHY–I have found that emerging Type 4s have oodles of empathy, and the real challenge for the adults in their lives is to help them learn to manage it. They will need to find a way to move out of feelings that can become too dark and heartbreaking and into action. Parents can help their 4 children with the following messages:

- "One day at a time."
- "How can you care for your heart?"
- "Let's go for a walk."
- "Let's say a prayer for that situation and release it to God."
- "Let's dance and move it out of our body."
- "Your feelings matter, now tell me about your thoughts."
- "Let's notice what's special about today."

Helping them internalize and grow true to these messages will result in self-talk that sounds like:

- "I can do hard things."
- "Everyone feels this way sometimes."
- "I can be present in this moment."

- "I don't have to believe every thought or feeling I have."
- "I can move my body and give my heart and mind a break."
- "I can generate ideas and take action."

Discipline

Disciplining a child with an emerging Type 4 personality will require you to do some creative thinking and careful parenting. Like 2s and 3s, these children wrestle with the Dragon of Shame and a fragile sense of worthiness. Again, connection comes first, and the message they should receive is that they are always valued and worthy of love, regardless of mistakes or dramatic outbursts.

I personally think it is best if consequences are action-oriented and done together. For example, you might say, "Because of your choice to …. I have decided that you will be helping me clean…" or "Since you and your brother were …, the two of you can … together." What we don't want to do with kids in the heart center is to send them to their rooms where their Dragon of Shame tells them they are being isolated as a form of rejection.

As they get older and need to manage their feelings, ask them to connect with their sensing body (1) and get moving into some kind of action, even if it is washing the dishes, going for a walk, or engaging in mindful breathing. Lead them to their thinking head (7) where their joy lives, and invite them to play or create, taking a break from the heaviness of emotions and having some fun.

Best Butterfly Self (1-4-7)

When 4s emerge as their best butterfly self, they will display the colors of creativity, sensitivity, intuition, and empathy as they help us see and appreciate the beauty in the world. When their harmony triad of 1-4-7 is integrated, the 4 can be found making an impact creatively. Think Joan Baez, or Prince, who both used their emotional sensitivities through artistry (4) and pushed what was possible in the industry (7) to deliver a message for social change (1) in their own unique way.

Suggestions for Parenting an Emerging 4

Parenting an emerging Type 4 child requires understanding their unique emotional depth, creativity, and desire for authenticity. Here are some suggestions to effectively nurture and support a Type 4 child.

- **Celebrate Their Uniqueness:** Type 4 children have a strong desire to be seen and appreciated for their individuality. Celebrate their uniqueness and encourage them to express themselves creatively. Provide opportunities for artistic expression, whether through art, music, writing, or other forms of self-expression. Acknowledge their distinctive perspective on the world and let them know that their feelings and thoughts are valid.

- **Foster Emotional Expression:** Type 4 children often have intense emotions, and it's essential to create a safe space for them to express and process these feelings. Encourage open and honest conversations about their emotions and validate their experiences. Teach them healthy ways to cope with strong emotions, such as journaling, mindfulness, or creative expression through art.

- **Support Their Need for Depth:** Type 4 children are drawn to deep, meaningful experiences and connections. Support their desire for depth by exposing them to literature, art, and philosophical discussions that resonate with their interests. Encourage them to explore their inner world and help them find meaning and purpose in their lives.

- **Teach Self-Compassion:** Type 4 children may be prone to self-criticism and feelings of inadequacy. Teach them self-compassion by emphasizing that it's okay to make mistakes and that self-acceptance is essential. Encourage them to treat themselves with the same kindness and understanding they offer to others.

- **Balance Independence and Connection:** Type 4 children may sometimes struggle with feelings of isolation. Help them strike a balance between their need for independence and their desire for connection with others. Encourage them to build meaningful relationships and to share their thoughts and feelings with trusted friends and family members.

- **Promote Healthy Self-Identity:** Type 4 children often grapple with questions of identity and self-worth. Foster their self-identity by helping them explore their interests, values, and passions.

Encourage them to embrace their authenticity and to be true to themselves rather than trying to conform to external expectations.

Remember, Type 4 children feel their emotions deeply. Help them remember to move their bodies and think things through as they take a pause from their feelings. They will need gentle reassurance that their sensitivity is a gift worth protecting and managing well.

THE HEAD CENTER TYPES:

5-6-7

CHAPTER 12

Fives

Meet William

One of five children, William was referred to me when he was 8 years old. His parents shared that he seemed angry and overwhelmed by the chaos and constant disruptions of his siblings. His parents feared that he was becoming walled off and distant and weren't sure if he was depressed.

Type 5: "The Investigator" (Head Center)

Type 5s are objective, focused, calm, and thoughtful. Healthy 5s are innovative and thirst for knowledge and can share it with empathy and action. They have an ability to concentrate and develop complex ideas and skills with keen attunement to the needs of society. 5s are not driven by social pressure but are individualistic, alert, and insightful, bringing calm wisdom to unfair situations. Healthy 5s observe and use knowl-

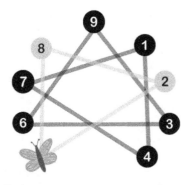

edge to act justly. They are called visionary pioneers as they are often ahead of their time and able to see the world in an entirely new way.

As a Child

Children with an emerging Type 5 personality are naturally curious and independent. They have an inherent thirst for knowledge and a desire to explore the world around them. These children often seek to understand complex concepts and may become engrossed in their intellectual pursuits. When facing their Dragon of Fear, a child with an emerging Type 5 personality might withdraw into their thoughts, becoming reserved and cautious. They may hesitate to engage in social situations or ask for help, preferring to rely on their own research and analysis to navigate challenging situations.

Kids displaying Type 5 personality traits may get feedback from others that they seem to be distant or cut off. As they grow older, you may be frustrated that they don't reply to your efforts to connect, ignoring messages and texts. At times, 5s can be very engaging and connected which leaves friends and family confused when they go "radio silent" as they retreat to their head.

As parents and important adults in the Type 5's life, we need to be patient as an overreach for connection will result in the opposite result. For example, when a Type 5 is protecting their energy, both physically and emotionally, we can say, "I would really like to connect with you," instead of, "Stop hanging out in your room and get out here."

At Their Core

At the core of a 5 is the desire to be competent and an intense fear of being inept. Their Dragon of Fear gets in their head with messages such as "Your needs are a problem," "Better figure it out on your own," "Neutralize the situation," and "You don't want to be seen as inadequate." It whispers to them that they need to conserve their energy, hoard their giftedness and limit connection to others lest they be overwhelmed. Their dragon flips the 5's strength of wisdom and invites them to get lost in a mind filled with thought after thought. It invites them to "hang out in here where it's safe," and like a turtle in a shell, they retreat.

Signs of Their Dragon

When 5s are overwhelmed by their Dragon of Fear, they withdraw and can become addicted to distance, often detaching themselves from others. They may guard their privacy and space in an effort to not be engulfed by others. During these times, they may become preoccupied with their thoughts and imagination. Fear can keep them attached to thinking and unable to process feelings. When on their edge, 5s can be intense and highly anxious and may even display the qualities of 7 seeming scattered, excitable, self-indulgent, and/or impulsive.

TRUE Parenting

TRUST-Raising an emerging 5 requires that you focus on building a strong foundation of trust. They will need to learn to tame their Dragon of Fear by learning how to balance their need to detach with staying connected. Remind them that you want to meet their needs and they are not alone in solving their problems. Help them get in touch with their body intelligence, helping them stay aware of physical indicators of stress and trusting their gut instincts. In order to grow true to their gifts encourage them to shift to their harmony strengths of Types 2 and 8. For example, when 5s are withdrawing, we can encourage them to connect to others (2) and courageously ask for what they need (8), reminding them that their needs are not a problem and that we're better when connected and facing challenges together.

RESILIENCE-Building resilience in a Type 5 must include caring for their body space as 5s are quick to disengage from sensation or instincts as a means to protect them-selves as they retreat into their world of thought. We want to help them feel safe in recognizing their needs and feelings while connecting to their own gut and emotional intelligence, integrating their harmony triad of 2-5-8.

UNIQUENESS–The goal here is to help your emerging Type 5 child learn that they don't have to conform and be like someone else. We want them to celebrate their main strength, wisdom, without arrogance, as they learn to integrate strengths from their other two centers. In their case, their intellect and resourceful thinking (5) can inform courageous action (8), especially when done in connection with the feelings of others (2).

EMPATHY–Parents can help their emerging 5 child build empathy for themselves and others by taming their Dragon of Fear with the following messages:

- "Your problems matter to me."
- "You don't have to handle this alone."
- "You can invite your feeling heart to help you connect to yourself and others."
- "You can take courageous action as you trust yourself."

Helping them internalize and grow true to these messages will result in self-talk that sounds like:

- "I can depend on others."
- "I can take action."
- "I can trust my gut."
- "I can stay connected and still meet my needs."
- "I can be creative in managing my energy."

Discipline

Parenting a child with an emerging Type 5 personality requires you to be sensitive to how you ask for connection. You will need to give your child space and ways to re-energize and not cause them to feel overwhelmed by the needs of the family.

Often, parents tell me that their Type 5 child is the one everyone wants to be with, but also the one who wants to be with everyone else the least, especially if they are introverted. It can be frustrating and difficult not to try to pull the 5 from their cave, as that is the exact action that causes them to double down and retreat. Allowing them space, and not putting them in a position to carry the emotional load, is key.

When an emerging Type 5 child is displaying behavior that requires discipline, it will be important for parents and caregivers to offer clear and consistent parenting. These kids want to know "why" and will be quick to give evidence for parent's failing to be fair in comparison to siblings or their own logic. If things "don't make sense," they may become argumentative and obstinate. As they battle fear, 5s may become anxious and worried, causing them to become more intense and impulsive.

These kids, like emerging 8s, will need loving adults who are calm and controlled in delivering consequences. They may also benefit from asking their child to offer suggestions on how to "make repair" to relationships or how they could do things differently in the future. This invitation to independent thinking and contribution to solving a problem is right up their alley and can go a long way in maintaining connection in times of friction.

As they grow older and face problem-solving situations, they will need assistance in processing their feelings. These children will benefit from methods that help them connect with their body (8) and their heart (2), enabling them to integrate their three centers in their 2-5-8 harmony triad.

Best Butterfly Self (2-5-8)

Emerging Type 5s, when healthy, will display vibrant qualities of wisdom, curiosity, and intellect. They will appear studious and possess skills for seeing the "big picture." They may become innovators in their field, demonstrating serious and focused intent. When operating from an integrated space, Type 5s can access the strength of the 8, taking courageous action to accomplish their goals while considering the needs of others with the compassion of a 2. Think of Marie Curie, who used her brilliant intellect to research groundbreaking scientific discoveries (5), taking courageous risks and actions (8) in her experiments and advocating for the welfare of humanity (2).

Suggestions for Parenting an Emerging 5

Parenting a Type 5 child requires understanding their natural inclination for curiosity, intellectual pursuits, and independence. Here are a few suggestions to nurture and support your emerging Type 5 child effectively:

- **Encourage Intellectual Exploration:** Emerging Type 5 children thrive on learning and intellectual discovery. Encourage their natural curiosity by providing access to books, educational resources, and opportunities to explore a wide range of subjects. Support their love of learning and help them develop their analytical thinking skills.

- **Respect Their Need for Independence:** Type 5 children value their independence and personal space. Respect their need for solitude and privacy, and provide a quiet, comfortable environment for them to think and create. Give them the freedom to pursue their interests and projects at their own pace.

- **Balance Independence with Social Interaction:** While Type 5 children may appear introverted and prefer solitary activities, it's important to help them balance independence with social interaction. Encourage them to engage in group activities, clubs, or hobbies where they can meet like-minded peers who share their interests.

- **Foster Emotional Expression:** Type 5 children may be reserved when it comes to expressing their emotions. Create a safe and non-judgmental space for them to talk about their feelings and experiences. Encourage them to express themselves through writing, art, or other creative outlets if verbal expression feels challenging.

- **Teach Effective Communication:** Type 5 children often excel in written communication but may struggle with verbal expression. Help them develop effective communication skills by practicing active listening and encouraging them to share their thoughts and ideas verbally. Teach them that their insights are valuable.

- **Support Healthy Boundaries:** Type 5 children may sometimes withdraw to avoid overwhelm. Encourage them to set healthy boundaries by recognizing when they need breaks or downtime. Teach them that it's okay to say "no" when they feel overextended or need space.

Remember, Type 5 children are naturally inquisitive with a thirst for knowledge. They are kids who can lead us with their wonder and curiosity about the world we live in. They need adults in their lives to nurture their gifts with opportunities to learn and explore while also helping them create strategies to maintain connection to themselves and others.

CHAPTER 13
Sixes

Meet Jack

Jack had just turned 8 when his Grandmother brought him in. She explained that his parents were separating and things had been a bit chaotic at home. Jack was exhibiting symptoms of anxiety that were keeping him up at night with worries about his family and endless questions of "what if?"

Type 6: "The Loyalist" (Head Center)

Type 6 Individuals are reliable, hardworking, and responsible. They are known for faithfully committing to their roles as friends and co-workers. Healthy 6s exhibit non-anxious vigilance. They are inquisitive and offer peaceful questioning. Type 6s look for danger or potential threats and anticipate where trouble might arise. Like a good boy or girl scout, they are alert, compassionate, and ready to help, especially with underdog causes.

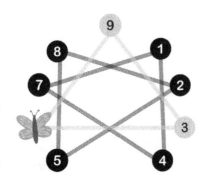

As a Child

Children with an emerging Type 6 personality are typically cautious and true-hearted kids. They have a strong need to feel safe and often seek guidance from trusted authority figures. These children are motivated by the

need for security and support. When struggling with their Dragon of Fear, an emerging Type 6 child may become overly anxious and indecisive, constantly seeking reassurance and overthinking potential dangers.

Emerging Type 6 kids often point out flaws in a plan or system that may be received by others as someone busting their balloon. As a parent, you may find yourself frustrated and think of them as a "joy kill" and "too negative," especially when you are trying to rally your family toward your idea.

Kids displaying Type 6 personality traits may get pushback from other adults and peers in response to their vigilance of what could go wrong and their constant need for consoling and encouragement that all is well. One of my adult clients, while exploring her childhood, said, "I can recall kids calling me a 'worry wart' and being amazed at my imagination of what might happen."

Parents and caregivers need to balance reassurance with truth, as kids can easily spot when someone is feeding them a line, which only increases their anxiety. These children want to feel prepared and have ideas about what might be needed or how to make things better. Share a little control by including them in finding solutions to their perceived problems and threats. Commend them for thinking of others, as they genuinely see things from a "what's best for everyone" point of view.

At Their Core

At the core of a Type 6 is a desire for security. Positioned in the middle of the Head Center, their Dragon of Fear distorts their thinking into an exercise of imagining what could go wrong. The messages they battle sound like: "What if?" "A lot could go bad!" "You better be prepared for things to go south," and "Be afraid. Be very afraid." Unlike other types, Type 6 individuals may respond to these messages in two opposing ways, either retreating or facing the perceived danger head-on. For example, imagine a Type 6 who is afraid of heights and either avoids flying or becomes a pilot.

Signs of Their Dragon

You will know a Type 6 is being overwhelmed by their dragon when they are either withdrawing to protect themselves or facing danger head-on. They may be fixated on worst-case scenarios and how to deal with them. In this state of overwhelm, 6s can be overly reactive, defiant, overly cautious, and highly anxious, operating from self-doubt and suspicion. Their usual cautiousness can escalate into overthinking and second-guessing themselves, leading to a state of perpetual worry. In stressful situations, a Type 6 might display a heightened need for structure and rules to regain a sense of security, and they may become defensive or confrontational when they perceive threats to their safety or stability. On this edge, 6s may move to the adaptive traits of Type 3 and may strive to get the recognition or approval of others, overwork, or perform with effort to deny and suppress their anxiety.

TRUE Parenting

TRUST–We want to help the emerging Type 6 child learn to trust all three centers of intelligence with an effort to honor and trust their ability to think, feel, and act. A Type 6 takes a "dependent stance" pattern of responding to the world and cares about how others see them. Building trust and providing them with a sense of "felt safety" is paramount to building a foundation of wellness and connection. It begins with you, but ultimately we want them to also learn to trust themselves.

When going through the "hard places," it will be vital to communicate plans and establish predictable routines when possible. As parents, we can encourage integration by guiding our emerging 6 children to shift to the butterfly strengths of types 3 and 9. We can help them set goals and make plans in small steps (3) and find ways to experience inner peace and harmony (9).

RESILIENCE–Building resilience in a Type 6 must include helping them learn to trust themselves and to do productive thinking. They will need a way to stop their inner hamster that runs on a "wheel of worry" and will benefit from lessons in connecting to their body through breath and mindful calming exercises.

UNIQUENESS–The goal here is to help your emerging Type 6 child learn that they don't have to conform and be like someone else; they get to celebrate their abilities to troubleshoot and to consider the greater good, which is important. When their questioning may not be well received, we want to help them learn to recover and remember that their worth is not tied to the opinions of others.

EMPATHY–Parents can help their emerging 6 child build empathy for themselves and others by taming their Dragon of Fear with the following messages:

- "You don't have to believe every story your mind comes up with."
- "You get to choose what you pay attention to."
- "You can turn off your head and connect with your body."
- "Thank you for thinking of the family or group. I've got it now."
- "You can trust me to take care of you."

Helping them internalize and grow true to these messages will result in self talk that sounds like:
- "I can trust myself and others."
- "I can take steps to problem-solve."
- "I can quiet my mind."
- "I can look inside for the answers."
- "I don't have to loop in the "what if" wheel."
- "I don't have to catastrophize things."

Discipline

Parenting a child with an emerging Type 6 personality requires managing your need for respect. Remember, trust is key, and connection is the goal. Like all children, these kids can become defensive when they get "in trouble" with their parents. However, a child displaying Type 6 behavior may dig their heels in a little deeper, asserting themselves and becoming skeptical of your ability to parent or lead.

Parents have shared with me that when questions begin, especially when attempting to discipline their children, they have a tendency to lose control and become angry as it feels like their authority is being questioned with tremendous disrespect. Again, parents need to remember that these kids need information for security.

"It may be helpful to remind your child that you love them and have been put in this role to protect and guide them. Let your parenting be consistent, and make your consequences clear while trying to remain calm in your conversation. If their tone of questioning becomes disrespectful, with comments like, "This is stupid..." "It doesn't make sense..." or "Why do I..." try to remember that you don't have to engage in this type of banter. Help them regulate their frustration and anxious thoughts, and remind them that you are the loving parent in charge. I used to say, "God made me your mom to love and teach you, and I'm doing my best."

When your child is calm, and all is said and done. You can have another conversation to answer lingering questions that offer reassurance and support for your child. You can say things like, "In this family, we ... " in support of the discipline you just issued. For example, "In this family, we respect each other and don't bully our siblings," or "To make sure you stay safe, we have a rule that you only get to use that tool with permission and supervision." This helps them see the "why" behind your actions, which goes a long way in building trust and credibility.

As they get older and need to manage their fear, ask them to engage in regulatory practices. It may be helpful to have a "calm down corner" in your home where they practice disengaging from anxious thoughts. Help them find inner peace (9) and strategies for acknowledging feelings and taking action (3). Suggest ways for them to take care of themselves proactively so that they can access these methods and find balance when their dragon invites them to spin in a whirlwind of imagined danger.

Best Butterfly Self (3-6-9)

When a child emerges as a Type 6 Butterfly, they beautifully display the vibrance of dependability, persistence, and vigilance. They radiate courage and loyalty, showing great devotion to their community, workplace, and loved ones. When their centers are integrated, the 6 can be found exhibiting the authentic side of the 9, showing peaceful contentment, and the productive side of the 3, taking effective action. Type 6 individuals are fascinating people who can uniquely hold space for both anxiety and courage. Think of Samwise from The Lord of the Rings, who was loyal and true (6), finding inner strength and commitment (9) to stay by his friend's side and take action every step of the way (3).

Suggestions for Parenting an Emerging 6

Parenting a Type 6 child involves recognizing their innate tendencies towards loyalty, responsibility, and a strong need for security. Here are some suggestions to effectively nurture and support your emerging Type 6 child:

- **Provide Reassurance:** Type 6 children often have concerns about safety and security. Offer reassurance and be a source of comfort when they express their worries. Let them know you're there to protect and support them.

- **Encourage Independence:** While Type 6 children may seek security, it's important to encourage them to develop independence and self-reliance. Gradually allow them to take age-appropriate risks and make decisions to build their confidence.

- **Teach Problem-Solving Skills:** Help your child develop problem-solving skills to navigate their anxieties and concerns. Teach them how to analyze situations and come up with practical solutions.

- **Model Trustworthiness:** Be a role model for trustworthiness and integrity. Demonstrate that your word can be relied upon. You do what you say you are going to do: you show up on time, you follow through with plans, and you don't over-promise, all of which helps them build trust in others and the world around them.

- **Create a Predictable Routine:** Establish a consistent daily routine and environment to provide a sense of stability and predictability. Knowing what to expect can help ease their anxiety.

- **Foster Open Communication:** Create an open and non-judgmental space for your child to express their fears and concerns. Encourage them to talk about their feelings and experiences and validate their emotions.

- **Teach them to Assess the Risks:** Help your child differentiate between real and perceived threats. Teach them to assess risks and make informed decisions rather than being overly cautious.

- **Promote Self-Esteem:** Build your child's self-esteem by acknowledging their achievements and capabilities. Encourage them to recognize their own strengths and abilities.

- **Expose Them to New Experiences:** Gently introduce them to new experiences and situations to expand their comfort zone. Gradual exposure can help them become more adaptable and less anxious about the unknown.

- **Provide Encouragement:** Offer words of encouragement and support when they face challenges or uncertainties. Let them know that you believe in their abilities and resilience.

Remember that Type 6 children value safety and security above all else and a strong relationship with you is built on trust. Providing a stable and supportive environment consistently while gently encouraging independence, you can help your developing Type 6 child thrive and grow true to their unique strengths and giftedness.

CHAPTER 14

Sevens

Meet Jonah

Jonah was referred to me when he was 14. A creative and active teen, Jonah's parents described their frustration at his lack of follow-through and constant activity. They were worried about his need to "always be on the move" and his refusal to talk about a recent family loss.

Type 7: "The Enthusiast" (Head Center)

Type 7s are versatile, optimistic, spontaneous, playful, high-spirited, and practical. They seek new and exciting experiences that bring life to themselves and others. Healthy Type 7s are visionaries who focus their talents on worthwhile goals. They are joyous, highly accomplished, and full of gratitude. Integrated Type 7s discover that joy includes living in the mundane and even in tragedy. They accept life as an adventure yet long to be grounded in what is most important.

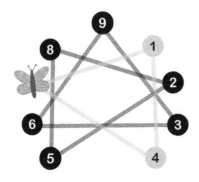

As a Child

Children with an emerging Type 7 personality are often imaginative and adventurous. They have an uncanny ability to reframe a negative into a positive in a "the sun will come out tomorrow" kind of way. When facing their Dragon of Fear, a child with an emerging Type 7 personality may display escapism, distractibility, avoidance, and fear of missing out. They may exhibit impulsive behavior and a constant pursuit of excitement and new experiences.

Children displaying Type 7 behavior may be coined "flighty" or get positive reinforcement for being funny and entertaining. They learn quickly to draw people to themselves through humor and a happy disposition.

These kids will need Parents and Caregivers who will give them space and opportunities to explore all of their feelings and learn to sit with the discomfort of "less fun" emotions like sadness and anger. Parents will need to watch for their avoidant behavior and moments when their emerging 7 children escape to the safety of their head space. Here, all things are possible, and the "hard places" are easy to reframe and ignore.

At Their Core

At the core of a 7 is the desire to have fulfillment. They fear being deprived and can be addicted to the need to be happy. In the Head Center, 7s battle the Dragon of Fear, which tells them to avoid pain and keep their options open. He tells them messages like, "Escape!" "Think of something you look forward to." "Fun is better than feeling." and "Pain is like going over a cliff." "Bring joy and make everyone's life better."

Signs of Their Dragon

When 7s are listening to their dragon, they can give signs of being scattered, impulsive, and avoidant. They may also appear to be restless, self-centered, overextended, and exhausted from always being on the go as they seek distractions. I've noticed in sessions that an emerging 7 child may begin to discuss real pain and then catch themselves and move toward statements like, "It's fine, though," or "Everything's good. It was a good day." "I have a lot to be thankful for." "At least..." Often, they are quick to focus on gratitude, enjoying the practice as a form of shifting attention from what might be wrong or painful. When under stress, they may exhibit traits of Type 1, becoming more self-critical and perfectionistic.

TRUE Parenting

TRUE–Emerging 7 children will need us to help them remember that they will be taken care of and that it's okay to depend on others. We want to teach them that fulfillment exists in experiencing the here and now and that they are capable of experiencing and staying with their full range of feelings.

As the adults in their lives, we can encourage our emerging Type 7 children to shift to the butterfly strengths of Types 1 and 4. For example, when struggling with avoidance, we can invite them to explore all their emotions (4). When they seem scattered and are doing too many things, we can help them shift to their responsible and diligent qualities (1).

RESILIENCE–Building resilience in a Type 7 must include embracing the full range of emotions. Kids in this space will require parents who help them feel safe to experience feelings of sadness, disappointment, frustration, and pain. They will need to learn that to live honestly means that they allow for a full range of feelings to be felt and expressed in a safe connection with those they love.

UNIQUENESS–The goal here is to help your emerging Type 7 child learn that they don't have to conform and be like someone else; they get to celebrate their main strength, joy, as they learn to integrate strengths from their other two centers. In their case, having optimism and a playful delight for life (7) can be balanced with making space to notice all their feelings (4) and staying the course to get things done diligently (1).

EMPATHY–Parents can help their emerging 7 child build empathy for themselves and others by taming their Dragon of Fear with the following messages:

- "You are only human, and life is sometimes hard."
- "You don't have to always be happy."
- "You can focus and do the right next thing."
- "You can follow through with one plan at a time."
- "You can trust others to support you in your pain."
- "You can find the strength and discipline to do hard things."

Helping them internalize and grow true to these messages will result in self-talk that sounds like:

- "I don't have to reframe everything."
- "I don't have to discount my feelings."
- "I don't need to protect others from my sad feelings."
- "I can stay grounded to what is most important."
- "I can find joy in the everyday moments of life."

Discipline

Parenting a child with an emerging Type 7 personality will require that you help them build structure and balance in their lives as they are pleasure seekers and may lack discipline to get the job done. These kids will need help to sit with pain and disappointment, which seems counterintuitive to most parents. It is easier to join them in the "glass is half full" mindset, but they will need us to help them avoid developing patterns of denial early. Notice when they share happy feelings and an upbeat attitude that doesn't fit the narrative of the current situation. Create a safe space for them to acknowledge their other emotions, if only for a little while.

You may discover that when disciplining a child who responds with, "Okay, that's fine… not a big deal," you might get defensive and feel the need to do more so your child "feels the consequence." Try to avoid reacting and recognize that it is just one of their ways of coping.

Usually, I hear from parents of older Type 7 kids who often tell me that their child is frustrating them because they "seem to be all over the place" and lack goals and direction. It will be important to teach them to follow through and finish what they started so they can reap the rewards of accomplishing something. As their interests diversify, guide them to greater balance where they can be more committed to their responsibilities.

Best Butterfly Self (1-4-7)

When a healthy Type 7 emerges, they radiate the colors of joy, optimism, creativity, spontaneity, and adventure. They are playful, action-oriented, and able to dream big while seeing the possibilities in every situation. Think of Elton John, a creative genius and consummate entertainer (7), diligent in perfecting his craft (1), and capable of embracing and eliciting every emotion (4).

Suggestions for Parenting an Emerging Seven

Parenting a Type 7 child requires understanding their natural inclination for adventure, exploration, and excitement. Here are a few suggestions to effectively nurture and support a Type 7 child:

- **Encourage Exploration and Creativity:** Foster their natural curiosity by providing opportunities for exploration and creativity. Allow them to pursue diverse interests and hobbies and expose them to a range of stimulating activities.

- **Balance Structure and Flexibility:** While Type 7 children may resist routines, help them strike a balance by setting clear expectations and boundaries. Provide a consistent daily routine and gently guide them toward completing tasks or responsibilities.

- **Foster Emotional Awareness:** Encourage emotional awareness and resilience by creating a safe space for them to express and process their feelings. Encourage and validate their expression of feelings, especially hard feelings on the other side of happiness.

- **Promote Responsible Decision-Making:** Teach them to make informed and responsible decisions, considering the consequences of their choices.

Help them understand that balance is essential, even in pursuit of excitement.

- **Set Realistic Goals:** Encourage them to set achievable goals and celebrate their accomplishments along the way. This helps them channel their enthusiasm into productive endeavors.

- **Model Healthy Risk-Taking:** Demonstrate healthy risk-taking by engaging in adventures and trying new things together as a family. Show them that calculated risks can lead to valuable experiences.

- **Provide Varied Experiences:** Introduce them to a wide range of activities, from outdoor adventures to cultural experiences. This keeps their curiosity alive and allows them to explore different interests.

- **Teach Gratitude:** Help them cultivate a sense of gratitude for the experiences and opportunities they have. Encourage them to appreciate the present moment and the people in their lives.

- **Balance Extravagance with Prudence:** If your child tends to be impulsive or excessive in their pursuits, guide them in making balanced decisions and considering long-term consequences.

- **Encourage Social Skills:** Type 7 children often enjoy socializing. Encourage the development of social skills, empathy, and the importance of building meaningful relationships.

- **Practice Mindfulness:** Teach mindfulness techniques to help them stay present and savor the experiences they encounter. Mindfulness can also help manage impulsivity.

- **Support Self-Reflection:** Encourage moments of self-reflection to help them understand their desires and motivations. This can promote self-awareness and personal growth while helping them avoid self-indulgence.

Type 7 children may be prone to impulsivity due to their desire for excitement. Teach them the importance of making thoughtful and informed decisions. Encourage them to consider the consequences of their choices and to pause and reflect before diving headfirst into new experiences. Help them develop a sense of responsibility for their actions while still embracing their adventurous spirit. Hold space with them when facing tough emotions and encourage them to experience all their emotions while protecting them from the pull of others who would resist this healthy expansion.

CHAPTER 15

Once Children

What's Next

We are now turning the corner toward answering that all-important question: "Now what?" Beyond all the wisdom of the Enneagram being reduced to memes and games on social media, the last thing I would want to see is parents and caregivers limiting their children in any way. I want to remind you that it is not your job to "type your child" but rather to be discerning about what dragon they are fighting and what brilliance they are beginning to shine.

Your mission is to be the parent your child needs to live into their true gifts and purpose, with the foundation of knowing they are brave and worthy of love and belonging. Remember, you can't lead your child down a road that you haven't traveled yourself, so your responsibility also extends to your own growth and well-being.

Once Children

There are times in conversation when I am asked, "What do you do?" Sometimes, I have gotten lost in my words to explain. "I am a therapist who works with children," and then I will add in a clumsy fashion, "...and adults. You know...people who were once children."

When I studied to become a therapist, I decided to specialize in helping children, and my first "real" job was as the children's therapist in a center for abused women. As a young therapist, it was a tough training ground. I always think of my time there in "dog years." A year felt like seven.

One day, while providing play therapy for two children, there came a knock on the door. It was another staff member summoning me into the hallway to quietly tell me some heartbreaking news. The young boy and girl playing with blocks on my office floor were suddenly without a mother. I learned that the children's mom, who had come into the shelter with a knife wound earlier, had been taken to the hospital and had died from internal bleeding. While other caseworkers did their best to find family members, I had to tell the children about their mother. I can't tell you how much that day shaped me.

Later, while attending this young mother's funeral, I was devastated to learn that she, like her children, had been a resident of the same shelter when she was a child. I was heartbroken and outraged. What! How? Why!? As a young therapist, I thought, "Wouldn't she have wanted something different?" and "Wouldn't that have taught her to go a different way?"

Again, theory and practice are two very different things. We may have the awareness and even the desire to approach our future differently than what we have experienced in our past. However, if we don't have help finding the way, we will default to our "automatic pilot" who will take us on an embedded course directed by our dragons of fear, shame, and anger.

I work with parents and caregivers every day who are trying to overwrite the downloads from childhood and kids who are actively trying to make sense of the messages coming in. All of them are trying to reclaim a part of themselves lost in childhood. It is the same work, just two sides of the spectrum.

Path of the Butterfly Keepers

There are times as a mom that I have felt like I am in a fastpitch batter's cage. School emails, dentist visits, homework, cheerleading practices, games, friends' birthday parties, and due dates all seem to be coming at me with great speed. And that's just the kid's stuff…when I add it to my pile of paperwork, caring for my clients, unexpected expenses, and pets, it's A LOT. Heaven forbid anyone gets sick! That really throws off the rhythm that's already on the edge of not being sustainable. If I'm honest, there is a part of me that enjoys the adrenaline that comes with the challenge, but most of me just feels exhausted.

We cannot continue to go along with the plan to hold our breath and white knuckle it until things get better. "I will do better" is not just a phrase. We get one shot for ourselves and our kids, and there is another way.

When I am connected to my nurturing heart, it beckons me to slow down, to take a breath, and to feel. In accepting this sacred invitation, time is suspended as I honor my heart and my body, which I have neglected for too long.

Reclaiming my authenticity while learning to live with Enneagram harmony has been a process and a practice.

It has been both refreshing and frustrating as I've had to learn a new way of living in connection with my three centers. Like trying to drive a stick shift for the first time, this process has not always been a smooth ride. At the same time, it has been the best and most worthwhile journey because it has been my path home to myself. I know the dragon that is showing up from time to time and I have the tools to face him. I no longer compare myself to others, at least I try not to, and I can acknowledge and display my own divine butterfly design.

We all deserve to live as our authentic best selves and to feel more content and alive. It's time to uncross your fingers and stop waiting for things to turn around on their own. There is a way for you to reclaim yourself and step into your personal growth process as you do.

Safe P.L.A.C.E.

I want everyone to know that though the ride may be bumpy, the work of becoming wholehearted is so worth it. To get there, each of us will need to be able to relate to ourselves from a safe place. Remember, we first learn how to do this as children with our early parents and caregivers. They are our Butterfly Keepers and nurture and support us by being playful, loving, accepting, curious, and empathetic.

You may or may not have had a healthy or attentive parent or caregiver. Perhaps someone was in your life physically but not attentive or attuned to your needs. Like orphans being given propped bottles, some of us were fed but not nourished. Maybe, like some of the children I serve, you had a parent or caregiver who not only failed to nourish you with love but actually hurt you. The desire you now have to nurture others may even come from this place of needing to be cared for yourself. I get it. It's how I came to adopt three children.

I want to encourage us to do our work first. Our dragons, like all of our children's dragons, are still here. Unlike a fairy tale, they cannot be destroyed. They can only be tamed and transformed. They will require our awareness and ongoing attention.

Get a Vision

We begin the transformation by getting a sense of where we are currently and plotting a course before us. It has been said that "those without vision perish." We must have some idea of where we would like to go before we can even hope to move from where we are. Here is one more tool you can use right away. When working with kids, I start with the zones of regulation.

I have no idea where these zones first originated. As a counselor, I have used them for years, though often, I have allowed kids to assign their own colors to each zone. You can do the same, but for now, let me introduce you to them as they are in my toolbox.

- **The Green Zone:** The Green Zone is our relaxed and happy zone. It is where we feel most like ourselves and where our emotions are regulated. In other words, we feel content being us in the world. Here, we are connected and focused. The green zone is where our butterfly comes out to play and enjoy life!

- **The Blue Zone:** The Blue Zone represents our state when we are experiencing less energy. We may be tired or "blue" and often attribute feelings such as sadness, melancholy, boredom, and/or loneliness.

- **The Yellow Zone:** In the Yellow Zone we are feeling more energy connected to adrenaline that comes with feelings of nervousness, anticipation, and anxiousness. We may feel "out of sorts" and scared as we begin to fear that we don't have as much control as we would like to have.

- **The Red Zone:** The Red Zone is often associated with anger, but it really is a zone where our energy is amped up. We may get this way when we are angry, but often, we can get really excited and "wired" when we experience other feelings, too.

As parents and caregivers, we can talk to kids about these zones with a focus on what it feels like to be there. We want to help them find words to describe how they experience each zone with attention to their three centers. We want to learn how to deal with this ourselves as a type of "inner parent" so that we can be more skilled at helping our kids.

We want to have them identify and label feelings, as well as notice their thoughts and body sensations. I like to ask: What zone do you think you're in? What feelings are you having? Where is your body holding them? What thoughts are you having? Are they helpful, true, and kind?

We want to teach our kids to navigate the zones with a special focus on creating conditions for the green zone with notice of their "best butterfly strengths." For example, it may sound like this:

- I'm noticing that you might be in the _____ zone?
- Can you tell me what's going on for you? Let's check in with your 3 centers.

- What are you feeling? Where in your body are you holding it? What do you need?
- Did you know we can all feel_____some-times, and I'm here for you?
- I'm just curious and want to help. I know you to be <u>(name their butterfly qualities)</u> What do you need to get back to being you?

Dragon Tales

When my kids were little, they loved to watch a series of movies called *Veggie Tales*. If you're unfamiliar, *Veggie Tales* was an animated series for children featuring Bob the Tomato and Larry the Cucumber. Crazy as it sounds, these vegetables effectively taught important lessons such as courage, forgiveness, and faith. Oh, and every lesson was also a musical! It's true...look it up.

The theme song was especially catchy. No matter how hard I tried, I couldn't seem to hit the pause button in my head on the sweet, bit obnoxious little tune. I'd try to fall asleep, and my mind would be singing, "Broccoli, Celery, Gotta be... Veggie Tales!" Between that and Barney, the early 2000s were rough.

Our "Dragon Tales" can be just as persistent but a lot less fun. As we've seen with each Type, they originate with the dragons of Fear, Shame, and Anger. And like a familiar tune, we can find ourselves humming along mindlessly, downloading their messages without taking the time to really evaluate their impact.

One of my favorite Viktor Frankl quotes tells us, "Between stimulus and response, there lies a space, and in this space lies our freedom and the power to choose." We want to be able to interrupt this dragon tale on auto-play and ask ourselves *what is it I'm actually believing?* What am I making an agreement with? In our mindful pause, we will make the choice, spread our wings, and take flight back to our true selves.

Noticing Patterns and Defense Strategies

From our position of being a safe PLACE for ourselves and our kids, we want to play detective and notice coping patterns and defense strategies that will clue us in on which dragon we are facing and which tool we need to tame it.

We want to do this with unconditional love and positive regard. We want to observe ourselves and our children. We want to teach our children to notice their own behaviors and patterns with compassion. We may do this by offering our own examples. It might sound like:

- "I was just realizing that I'm in the Blue Zone and feeling a little down today."
- "I think I'll take care of myself by going on a walk. Would you like to join me?"
- "Ugh, my dragon is trying to get me to worry. I am going to check… is that thought true? Is it kind? Is it helpful?
- "I can feel my heart racing in my body. I will take care of it by doing some rainbow breathing."

Wholehearted Connections

Integrating our three centers of intelligence and shifting focus to return to our authentic selves is not about grit or tenacity. Our children need real tools to help them calm activated nervous systems operating in response to the dragons of fear, shame, and anger. We must help them make 'wholehearted connections' that support their best butterfly self and practice mastering these strategies in connection to us.

I have a series of activities and creative means to help kids learn how to calm their bodies and shift their thinking. "Rainbow Breathing," "Magic Mustache," and "Calm Down Jars" are just a few ways I help kids practice strategies to tame their dragons and their nervous systems. You can download these and many others for free on my website. They are best learned in playful connection with you, the parent, or a safe caregiver.

Lather. Rinse. Repeat.

Becoming wholehearted, that is, learning to live as those who know they are brave and worthy of love and belonging, is a never-ending practice. It is wonderful and hard, liberating and overwhelming. But it is the practice we use to grow in our truth. We can either take a quick bite like a mom grabbing leftovers from her child's plate, or we can find a seat at the table and begin to nourish our souls.

It will be our daily practice. Stay open, my friend. Stay compassionate. Fall down. Get up and try again.

CHAPTER 16
Note to Self

It's important that we recognize what we are bringing to the table regarding our own Enneagram lens and parenting. Let's take a brief look at the type 9s as parents.

As Parents

8s–Type 8 parents are known for their assertiveness, strong-willed nature, and desire for control. They often approach parenting with a sense of responsibility and may lead with a "take-charge" role within the family. They can be overprotective, excessively worried about sheltering their kids, and strict in setting boundaries and enforcing the rules. It is important that they work to allow open communication with their children, avoid becoming a dictator, and allow their kids to express themselves and have their own feelings and opinions. It will be vital that the Type 8 parent manages their anger and impatience, creating a sense of "felt safety" within their home and family relationships. Growth in Type 8 parents looks like integrating their centers within the harmony triad, 2-5-8.

9s–Type 9 parents are known for their easygoing and peaceful nature. They often bring a sense of calm and nurture to the family environment, which lends a sense of harmony and stability. They avoid conflict and can see both sides of every situation, which may cause some frustration for their parenting partner when making tough parenting decisions. To support their role as parents, Type 9 parents can work on assertiveness and self-expression, ensuring that their needs and concerns are acknowledged within the family dynamic. They can also benefit from setting clear boundaries and providing structure for their children while still engaging in open communication and healthy conflict resolution. Growth in Type 9 parents looks like integrating their centers within the harmony triad, 3-6-9.

1s–Type 1 parents are known for their conscientious approach to parenting as they have a strong desire to provide structure and discipline, often with a moral code, for their children. These parents worry about their children as well as themselves, at times with an undertone of perfectionism and critical voice. They worry about "getting it right" as parents and are concerned that a misstep in their parenting could lead to disastrous results. Type 1 parents can support their role by practicing flexibility and self-compassion. They can also benefit from being open to sharing and receiving support from trusted friends and family members, as well as creating balance in themselves and family. Growth in Type 1 parents looks like integrating their centers within the harmony triad, 1-4-7.

2s–For Type 2s, caregiving and parenting are their jam! Nurturing and empathizing come easily to them, and they desire emotional connection with their children above all else. Type 2 parents tend to worry and over-perform, often allowing their child's emotional well-being to eclipse their own. It will be important for them to consistently set clear boundaries and expectations, as well as follow through on consequences. Type 2 parents need to keep an eye on their own needs and health, both emotional and physical, so they can be the parents their children require. Growth in Type 2 parents looks like integrating their centers within the harmony triad, 2-5-8.

3s–Type 3 parents approach parenting with a focus on success as they strive to raise accomplished children. They are concerned with their children's performance and have a strong need to project an image of perfection to the outside world. They might also over-identify with their kids and their success, so it is vital that they disconnect their worth as parents from their children's outcomes. It is also important that their kids feel loved for who they are and not for what they achieve. Unconditional love is key. They should make sure to allow their child the freedom to be themselves and set realistic expectations and goals together. Prioritizing connection and open communication is essential. Growth in Type 3 parents looks like integrating their centers within the harmony triad, 3-6-9.

4s–Type 4 parents are known for their emotional sensitivity and often approach parenting with a commitment to nurture their child's uniqueness and self-expression. They may be especially attuned to signs of distress or emotional unrest in their children and struggle with their own confidence as parents. A Type 4 parent will benefit from encouraging open communication and actively listening to their child's thoughts and feelings. Strongly empathetic, Type 4 parents will need to work hard at setting boundaries and helping their children problem solve and develop tools to deal with life's challenges. Growth in Type 4 parents looks like integrating their centers within the harmony triad, 1-4-7.

5s–Type 5s bring their love for knowledge to their role as parents, seeking information and strategies to ensure they make the best decisions for their kids. It is important for Type 5 parents to focus on staying connected with their children and not detaching when they don't feel as competent as they think they should be. Type 5 parents need to allow themselves to make mistakes and remember that the best parenting practices come from staying engaged. Growth in Type 5 parents looks like integrating their centers within the harmony triad, 2-5-8.

6s–Type 6 parents may struggle with worry and excess concern for their child's well-being and safety. They may battle an active imagination with potential dangers and scenarios that place their child in harm's way. Their concerns can lead to overthinking and sometimes micromanaging their child's life. It may help Type 6 parents to focus on nurturing a sense of security and trust within the family. Building a support network of friends and family can help alleviate some of their worries, providing them with different perspectives and reassurance when needed. Practicing mindful based stress reduction will help in managing their "hamster on a wheel" spinning mind. Growth in Type 6 parents looks like integrating their centers within the harmony triad, 3-6-9.

7s–Type 7 parents are known for their fun-loving and adventurous spirit. They approach parenting with a desire to create a connection with their children through joy and fun experiences. They worry about keeping their children happy and want their lives to be filled with good memories. Type 7 parents can struggle with consistency, boundaries, and structure. They may need to develop in these areas so their kids can enjoy a balance of fun, healthy discipline, and responsibility. Growth in Type 7 parents looks like integrating their centers within the harmony triad,1-4-7.

Awareness is our first step in the growth process of becoming the parents our children require. As we recognize our children's patterns, as well as our own, we will be able to connect with greater intentionality and sincerity.

Conclusion
Training Wheels

When I was little, I counted on my red Hush Puppy sneakers to take me anywhere. I loved them, and I loved to play and explore. On my 7th birthday, I was given a new mode of transportation: a bright royal blue bicycle embedded with sparkles. It had a white basket to hold my doll and tassels in various colors that I used to represent the flavors of imaginary ice cream that I sold to my sister and neighborhood friends.

That day, as my mom cleaned up the discarded wrapping paper, my dad was hunched over my new gift, attaching the training wheels. Hyped up on birthday cake, I twirled around and tossed my hair back like Cher to "I Got

You Babe," playing on a little transistor radio in our garage. I waited, somewhat impatiently, for my chance at freedom.

When I finally hopped on, to my surprise, freedom wasn't immediate. My dad was there. He had put the training wheels on a bit high so they only made contact if I really needed them. So, instead of launching my solo ride with grace and speed, my Dad jogged next to me, coaching me while holding onto my seat.

"Push down, but look up," I could hear him say. "Watch where you're pointing the wheel." "Keep going... You can do it." "Now, brake, brake!"

It wasn't long before the training wheels came off, and I was taking off. By third grade, my dad traded that sparkly blue bike for a canary yellow ten-speed Schwinn. It was huge, and even with my long "spider legs," the seat was too high for me to use and reach the pedals. But I loved it and rode everywhere, even with the seat hitting me in the back.

Learning to Fly

I grew into my bike and, although I crashed pretty hard a few times, I never thought about my first training wheels or my dad's words again until now. I realize that his words were always guiding me as I grew. I know now when to push and how to keep my head up and steer toward the direction I want to go. His lessons and my experience with my training wheels supported my new adventure and growth.

As parents and caregivers, we don't give training wheels to kids and say, "Here-this will help you. Enjoy!" Rather, we put them on and guide them as they learn to navigate and grow in their independence. *The Wholehearted Child* is your opportunity to put training wheels on your child's development, allowing them to receive your guidance and instruction. It is a means to help them grow into the best version of themselves and to enjoy the adventure of living.

Throughout this book, I have provided insight into how our early attachment relationships give birth to our ego dragons, shaping a lens or script about ourselves and our place in the world. I have introduced you to these families of dragons named Anger, Shame, and Fear, and given you some patterns to look for in yourselves and your children.

Some of you may not have had parents who emotionally provided you with training wheels, and you may have habits to change, like stopping with your feet. You are now invited to be an observer of self with non-judgment and self-compassion so you can lead your kids to do the same.

Hopefully, throughout this book, you have recognized your own dragon, and you will know when you're in its presence. My hope for you is that you will also know how to discern its lies and interrupt your reactivity with Enneagram-informed strength and wisdom.

There is a little poem that I think applies to all of us. After all, we all have a childhood that impacts our adulthood. It reads, "In life, children need just two things. First, they need roots, and then they need wings."

My prayer is that you can reclaim your childhood roots and remember you were created to soar with brilliant colors and the divine gifts the world needs. This may require engaging in your own personal growth process with courage and compassion.

By nurturing your own growth, you can create the conditions for yourself to thrive. From this place, you will be able to fully live your one wild and precious life as you lead your child to do the same.

GLoSSARY oF TERMS

Adaptive Self: The adaptive self represents the aspects of an individual's personality and behaviors that have developed as coping mechanisms to navigate life's challenges.

Attachment: Attachment refers to the deep emotional bonds and connections that individuals form with others, typically starting in childhood. It encompasses the ways people seek closeness and security in their relationships.

Attachment Theory: *Definition:* Attachment theory is a psychological framework developed by John Bowlby that examines the emotional bonds formed between children and their caregivers and how these bonds influence personality and relationships throughout life.

Attachment Therapist: An attachment therapist is a mental health professional who specializes in addressing attachment-related issues and helping individuals build secure and healthy emotional connections.

Authentic Self: The authentic self represents the true and genuine essence of an individual, free from pretense or societal expectations.

Brene Brown: Brene Brown is a research professor and author known for her work on vulnerability, shame, courage, and empathy. Her research has had a significant impact on understanding human emotions and connections.

Butterfly Self: The "Butterfly Self" is a term that is used to describe our most authentic and true self.

Butterfly Keeper: The "Butterfly Keeper" is a term that is used to describe parents and caregivers who have the incredible responsibility of caring for children and safeguarding their development.

Centers of Intelligence: In the context of the Enneagram, the Centers of Intelligence refer to the three groups of personality types (Head, Heart, and Gut) that are associated with distinct patterns of thinking, feeling, and reacting.

Childhood: Childhood is the early period of a person's life, typically from birth to adolescence, characterized by significant physical, emotional, and cognitive development.

Childhood Development: Childhood development encompasses the physical, cognitive, emotional, and social growth and changes that occur in individuals from birth through adolescence.

Dan Siegel (referring to Dr. Daniel J. Siegel): Dr. Daniel J. Siegel is a psychiatrist and author known for his work in interpersonal neurobiology and the development of the "mind-sight" approach to understanding the mind and relationships.

Ego: The ego is a psychological concept representing a person's conscious self-identity and sense of self-importance. It can also refer to the part of the mind that mediates between the conscious and unconscious.

Enneagram: The Enneagram is a personality system that describes nine distinct personality types, each with its own motivations, fears, and behaviors. It is often used for self-discovery and personal growth, as well as a tool for understanding and improving relationships.

Erik Erikson: Erik Erikson was a developmental psychologist known for his theory of psychosocial development, which outlines a series of stages individuals go through from infancy to adulthood, each characterized by specific challenges and outcomes.

EQ (Emotional Intelligence): Emotional Intelligence (EQ) is the ability to recognize, understand, manage, and effectively use one's own emotions and those of others. It plays a crucial role in interpersonal relationships and social interactions.

False Self: The false self refers to a persona or identity that individuals may adopt to meet societal expectations or mask their true emotions and vulnerabilities.

Gut Intelligence (GQ): Gut Intelligence, often referred to as GQ, is a term in the Enneagram system that represents a person's innate intuitive sense, instincts, and visceral reactions to situations.

Hard Places: "Hard Places" is a term that was often used by Dr. Karyn Purvis to describe challenging or difficult life experiences, particularly those that can impact an individual's attachment style, as well as their emotional and psychological wellness.

Harmony Triads: The Harmony Triad is a term within the iEnneagram system that refers to the combinations of Head-Heart-Gut intelligence that correlate and provide guidance for one's personal growth. These include triads 1-4-7, 2-5-8, and 3-6-9.

iEnneagram (Ignatius Enneagram): The iEnneagram is a specific aspect of the Enneagram system that focuses on the process of personal growth and development by integrating the three centers of intelligence.

Ignatius (referring to Saint Ignatius of Loyola): Saint Ignatius of Loyola was a Spanish priest and theologian who founded the Society of Jesus (Jesuits) and developed the Spiritual Exercises. His work focuses on spiritual growth, discernment, and self-examination.

Inner Child: The inner child represents the childlike aspects of a person's psyche and emotions. It often refers to unresolved childhood emotions, memories, and needs that continue to influence adult behavior and emotions.

Inner Critic: The inner critic represents the internal voice that often provides self-criticism and negative self-judgment, influencing one's self-esteem and self-worth.

Integration (in the context of the Enneagram): Integration, in the Enneagram, represents a state in which an individual adopts positive qualities of their harmony triad, allowing them to live.

Intentionality: Intentionality is the quality of being deliberate and purposeful in one's thoughts, actions, and decisions. It involves setting clear intentions and aligning actions with those intentions.

IQ (Intelligence Quotient): IQ is a measure of a person's cognitive abilities, often assessed through standardized tests. It is used to evaluate a person's intellectual potential and problem-solving skills.

John Bowlby: John Bowlby was a British psychologist and psychoanalyst known for his groundbreaking work in the field of attachment theory. He developed the theory of attachment to understand the importance of early emotional bonds between children and their caregivers.

Karyn Purvis: Karyn Purvis was a developmental psychologist and expert in attachment and trauma, known for her work in Trust-Based Relational Intervention (TBRI) to support children who have experienced trauma and attachment issues.

Maladaptive Behavior: Maladaptive behavior refers to actions, habits, or coping mechanisms that are harmful or counterproductive to an individual's well-being.

Mindfulness: Mindfulness is a practice of being fully present and attentive to the current moment without judgment. It is often used to reduce stress, improve focus, and enhance emotional well-being.

Mindset: Mindset refers to a person's beliefs, attitudes, and mental frameworks that shape their perception of themselves and the world. It can be categorized as either a fixed mindset or a growth mindset.

Narrative: Narrative refers to the stories and interpretations that individuals create to make sense of their experiences, shaping their understanding of themselves and the world.

Personal Narrative: Personal narrative is an individual's unique life story, encompassing their experiences, memories, and the meaning they ascribe to their journey.

Patterns: Patterns refer to recurring behaviors, thoughts, or actions that individuals exhibit in response to specific situations or triggers.

Secure Attachment: Secure attachment is a healthy and positive emotional bond formed between a child and their caregiver, providing a sense of trust and security.

Self-Aware: Being self-aware means having a deep understanding of one's own thoughts, emotions, behaviors, strengths, weaknesses, and motivations.

ABOUT THE AUTHOR

Susan Parker Jones is a seasoned professional with over 25 years of experience as a licensed counselor, author, and trainer with focus on healing the "hard places" of childhood.

Through the creation of her signature program, "Wholehearted Connections," Susan has demonstrated a profound commitment to helping children and families thrive, recognizing that the path to self-discovery and healing is an ongoing journey.

Susan's expertise extends to being a certified TBRI (Trust-Based Relational Intervention) practitioner and trainer, where her work in trauma-informed care has provided crucial support to individuals and families navigating complex challenges. She also holds certifications as a Coach through the REALIFE Process and Motions of the Soul, highlighting her ongoing commitment to growth and learning.

In *The Wholehearted Child*, she draws upon her extensive experience and steadfast dedication to guide readers on a transformative journey toward self-discovery and enneagram informed parenting. Her wisdom and compassionate understanding shine through in her words, offering an invaluable resource for those who seek personal growth while making a meaningful impact on the lives of the next generation.

To obtain tools to enhance your skills as a "Butterfly Keeper" and/or to begin the journey of strengthening your "Wholehearted Connections," visit Susan at susanparkerjones.com

A free ebook edition
is available with the
purchase of this book.

To claim your free ebook edition:

1. Visit MorganJamesBOGO.com
2. Sign your name CLEARLY in the space
3. Complete the form and submit a photo of the entire copyright page
4. You or your friend can download the ebook to your preferred device

A **FREE** ebook edition is available for you or a friend with the purchase of this print book.

_____

CLEARLY SIGN YOUR NAME ABOVE

Instructions to claim your free ebook edition:
1. Visit MorganJamesBOGO.com
2. Sign your name CLEARLY in the space above
3. Complete the form and submit a photo of this entire page
4. You or your friend can download the ebook to your preferred device

Print & Digital Together Forever.

Snap a photo   Free ebook   Read anywhere